Fun and Easy Ways to Teach Your Toddler to Write

135+ Activities, Resources, and Tips for Teaching Writing with Play

---

ANDREA STEPHENSON

www.SimplyOutrageousYouth.org
amills@SimplyOutrageousYouth.com

DEDICATION

To Lyndon,

Thank you for always encouraging me in my endeavors. You have pushed me to put my materials and expertise out to the world to help others. You have adjusted so I can make my dreams of writing and being a strong presence in our son's life come true. Thank you for being you. Let's continue to do this life together!

I love you,

Andrea

REVIEWS

This is a fantastic, thoughtful resource for anyone who wants to give their child a head start for school as well as cultivate a love for learning. It gives parents or caregivers who want to spend quality time with their child clear instructions and a wide variety of activities so they can strengthen their bond and create lasting memories with their child while teaching them valuable skills and having fun. An indispensable resource for those with young children!

—Stacey K., editor and mother of 4

This book is a fantastic resource for parents and educators in the midst of teaching their children literacy skills. It provides excellent activities, book references, and resources to teach toddlers how to write, along with educational insights regarding children's brain development and cognition. I love how Andrea uses fun and creative literacy techniques to instill an early love of learning in young children. As a mom of two toddlers, I am excited to use these engaging techniques with my girls!

—Amber F., mom of two toddlers.

ABOUT ME

Hello, and thank you for purchasing my book! My name is Andrea Stephenson, and I am a wife and the mommy of a curious, energetic four-year-old boy!

I am a Licensed Clinical Social Worker who created the Simply Outrageous Youth (SOY) organization. SOY was created because of the need to teach our children life skills using fun and hands-on methods.

When I was young, my family used games, role playing, and real-life experiences to teach me various life lessons. For example, my older brother taught me about credit and the stock market through a game he created called Traders.

Once I became a mom, I wanted to create these same experiences for my son and children around the world.

I have done extensive research on how kids' brains develop and how to engage them in fun learning methods even as babies.

When my son was born, I constantly played and interacted with him to create a strong bond. I saw how much he loved learning. This interaction coupled with my research resulted in him writing his first letter and beginning to spell at twenty-one months.

This book was written to show you exactly how this was done without worksheets and flashcards. It was all done through **play**!

Believe me, it was not my intention to teach him how to write at such an early age. I didn't think he would learn to write until the age of five.

I followed my child's lead in him wanting to absorb more knowledge, and I used the social worker mantra when dealing with others, which is, "Meet them where they are."

You will see that I have used fun activities to expose my son to forming shapes, letters, and numbers. For example, playing with Play-Doh and building with Legos were used to teach my son to write.

My purpose is to open your eyes to a new way of learning. Learning can take place anywhere. Just think of our planet as a big learning playground.

Let's start this fun adventure together!

ANDREA STEPHENSON

www.SimplyOutrageousYouth.org

Amills@SimplyOutageousYouth.com

Follow Simply Outrageous Youth on:

YouTube

Pinterest

Facebook

Instagram

Make the world a learning playground for you and your child.

— Andrea Stephenson

Contents

CHAPTER 1

How Did You Get Your Son to Write at Two Years Old?

HOW DID YOU GET YOUR SON TO WRITE AT TWO YEARS OLD?

When I First Noticed

While cooking one day, I gave my one-year-old son, Cory, paper and crayons so he could create a masterpiece. I expected him to scribble on the paper and make beautiful abstract art deserving of my compliments. He exceeded my expectations with this task. I looked at the paper and saw circular shapes, lines, scribbles, and the letter *A*. I quickly took a picture with my cellphone and said, "Wow, you wrote an *A*!" This picture was shown to my husband and immediately sent to family members.

If you look at the picture below, it is hard to tell where the *A* is written because he wrote over it. However, I made circles around the *A*'s to more easily identify them. Knowing how much my child has viewed the alphabet in books, during playtime, while watching television, and while watching me write letters, there was no doubt in my mind that he was starting to write.

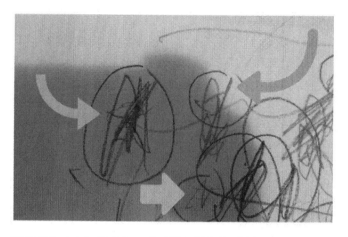

This is my son's artwork. I first noticed him writing his first set of A's at one year old. I circled the A's with a crayon.

Plenty of Opportunities to Write

We especially love all the seasons because they give us opportunities to play in different ways. During the spring, summer, and fall, we go outside to play on the playground and then head to the blacktop in our neighborhood for more fun. Before going outside, I carry a red backpack equipped with bubbles, a ball, and sidewalk chalk. While at the blacktop, our normal routine is to blow and catch bubbles, kick or catch the ball, and then create art and write with sidewalk chalk. **I remember observing my son writing the whole alphabet and numbers from one to one hundred as a two-and-a-half-year-old.**

Cory writing numbers 1-100 with sidewalk chalk at 2.5 years old.

Wintertime also offered writing opportunities because we could take a stick and form letters and numbers in the snow. It was also a time where we did fun activities inside that honed my son's writing skills.

Writing Notes

I like to expose my son to learning in various ways. Once Cory started reading sentences independently, at the age of two, sometimes instead of verbally telling him to do something, I would write it on his doodle pad. The sentences I wrote were short and simple, such as, "Please say goodnight to Daddy." If I wanted him to reply to me, I would ask a question like, "Did you have fun today?" Cory would write, "Yes." During the summer of his second year, as we were driving to Busch Gardens, the amusement park, he wrote the words, "So fun," on his doodle pad.

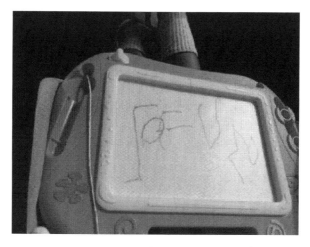

On our way to an amusement park, my son wrote the words, "So fun" when he was two years old.

The doodle pad made written communication fun for my son. It was a platform for him to draw and quickly erase as his mind thought of something else to write. As we explored museums, amusement parks, and various play areas, he saw letters everywhere in signs, advertisements, directions, etc. Cory was amazed that he had the ability to create those same letters on the doodle pad. We took it everywhere to keep him occupied, including restaurants, waiting rooms, and church.

Writing Greeting Cards to Others

Once I saw that Cory liked writing, I wanted to give him more opportunities to do it. When it was a family member's or friend's birthday, he created greeting cards for them. He also wrote thank-you cards when he received gifts. Knowing that we were sending his card to another person fascinated him. The materials used were colorful construction paper, crayons, and markers. If it was his grandmother's birthday, I would write on a separate piece of paper, "Happy Birthday, Grandma," with lines underneath each word. The purpose of doing this was to show him that a word would go on each line. After he chose a particular color construction paper to write on, I would draw the lines on paper so he could write his letters on them.

He would write "Happy" on the first line, "Birthday" on the second line, and "Grandma" on the third line. On the back, Cory would draw a picture or write his alphabet and numbers. The positive response of family members and friends after getting their birthday and thank-you cards in the mail made my son feel so proud. Some family members sent him a video holding the card he made and thanking him for taking the time to create it.

This is also a great money saver! He gets invited to a lot of birthday parties. Instead of buying a card, he just creates one of his own. Once we get to the party, he is so excited to share his work that he insists on giving the birthday boy or girl their card as soon as we arrive.

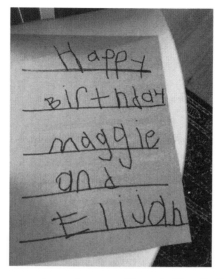

Cory beginning to make a card for his friends' birthday.

How Long Did It Take?

I believe Cory started learning to write the first time he saw the alphabet and numbers. His brain was taking mental pictures of how the letters were formed through seeing words and numbers in books and within our play. We will expand on this later in the book.

As mentioned earlier, I first noticed my son write the letter *A* within his picture of scribbles at twenty-one months. By the age of two and a half or thirty months, he was writing the full alphabet (uppercase letters) and numbers outside with sidewalk chalk. It took about nine months but I think the SCIENCE of learning to write though PLAY accelerated his pace. We will discuss the science of learning to write in the next chapter.

TIP #1

Encourage your child to use crayons and markers to create art.

TIP #2

The more exposure your child has to viewing the alphabet, numbers, and shapes, the better their writing will become.

TIP #3

Give your child various opportunties and settings in which to write.

CHAPTER 2

The Science Behind Learning to Write

THE SCIENCE BEHIND LEARNING TO WRITE

Part of learning to write is to remember how letters, shapes, and numbers are formed. Most children are taught this through tracing letters, numbers, lines, and shapes repeatedly. Although this is very effective, there are other science-proven tricks that can accelerate the learning process and make it fun.

Picture Things

Picturing information makes it much easier to remember. For example, if you ask a child what is in their bedroom, their first action is to picture their room in their mind and visualize what is there. The right side of the brain is driven by feelings, beliefs, imagination, and subjective thinking. It is creative and processes visuals well. However, the left side of the brain is logical, analytical, attentive, and rational. It processes language, facts, science, and math well.

So how do you remember information better?

You incorporate both the right- and left-brain strengths into learning. **One way to do this is to convert a fact into a picture, so you can remember it more easily.** If the picture is strange or unusual, it is easier to remember. Additionally, if the picture involves movement, then it makes the connection stronger.[1]

Let's use a letter and number as an example. If your child is learning to write the letter *A*, you may want to connect it with a picture of a triangle. While tracing or showing them how to write it, tell your child the *A* is part triangle with a line in the middle. It is important to use what is familiar to your child for the picture. In other words, ensure the child knows what a triangle and line look like. If they don't know, then use another picture such as stick man legs with a line in the middle.

⋀ This is part triangle.

A This is part triangle with a line in the middle called an A.

You may also describe an *A* as stick man legs with a line in the middle.

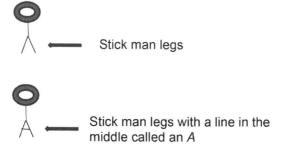

Stick man legs

Stick man legs with a line in the middle called an *A*

[1] Barbara Oakley PhD, Terrane Sejnowski, PhD. "Learning How to Learn: A Guide for Kids and Teens."

If you are teaching your child to write the number 5, then you may create the image in their mind that it is a man with a big belly wearing a hat. Let's look at the example below.

$$5 \longleftarrow \text{Hat}$$
$$\longleftarrow \text{Big belly}$$

As your child is tracing or you are showing them how to write, use the words to describe the picture of the letter or number you want to put in their mind.

I created a picture for every letter, number, and shape my son wrote. Then when he started writing independently, I would describe the picture to him. For instance, when he first learned to write the letter *B*, he would say the following, "Line down with a big belly on top and big belly on the bottom."

$$\text{Line down} \longrightarrow B \longleftarrow \text{Big belly}$$
$$\longleftarrow \text{Big belly}$$

Make Up Songs

Songs are a great way to remember new information. When I ask parents about activities their young children like to do, their answer is most often listening to music, dancing, and playing. So why not apply it to writing? First use a song to get your child familiar with their letters and numbers. While there is a lot of great music out there, I highly recommend listening to toddler radio stations on any digital musical outlets like Pandora. Also, I love the hip-hop album from Mark D. Pencil entitled *Learning with Hip-Hop.* Their songs assisted in teaching my son the alphabet, to count to one hundred, and how to count by twos, fives, and tens.

Now it is time to make up a song as you are teaching your child to write. An example of a song for the numbers would be,

> *Number 1 is a long line named Don*
> *Then there is 2, who looks like a Swan*
> *Here comes 3, the two backward C's*

The song does not have to rhyme. It can be created with the words used to describe pictures.

Metaphors

Coming up with creative metaphors is one of the best ways to learn a new concept or share ideas. Metaphors are similarities between the object or information you want to remember and something you already know. Metaphors activate brain links that allow a child to do more complex thinking about a real concept. This relates to the *neutral reuse theory*, which means you are using ideas you are familiar with to learn new knowledge.

While teaching your child to write the letter *C*, you can tell them it looks like a crescent moon. Writing the letter *C* is what they need to remember, but the moon is something they are familiar with. Take it a step further by showing them a picture of a crescent moon.

When creating metaphors, think of a child's imagination. The funnier, weirder, and wackier a metaphor is, the better. For example, the letter *C* can look like the giant sideways smile of a monster. The lowercase *d* may resemble a man with a ball stuck to his foot. We tend to remember things that are simply outrageous!

Imagination

Children have excellent imaginations. I believe imagination is at its peak level during childhood. Let's use it to help children learn to write by having them imagine they are a letter or number they are learning to write. Show your child a picture of the letter *E* and ask them, "What it is like to be this letter?" If they don't understand this question, ask them, "What does an *E* look like?" A child may say it looks like a snake with three arms or a sideways table. When I ask my son what the letter *M* reminds him of, he says it looks like a monster. Whatever they come up with, it is correct. I expanded on his thoughts and said, "Then *M* is a monster that moves up, down, up, and down.

down up

up **M** down

If they are still having trouble answering your question, then use an answer they previously gave to help them write other letters. The letter *F* could be a snake with two arms instead of three (like *E*). This could also be a time to do some creative or silly story-telling or writing. Below is an example starting with the letter *G*:

Once there was a G *that carried a* C *and backward lowercase* r.

He didn't want to carry r *because he wanted to jump over the letter* H.

H *was made of two large sticks carrying one small stick.*

If G *jumped over* H, *then the small stick would be scared.*

C ⟶ **G** ⟵ Backward
lowercase *r*

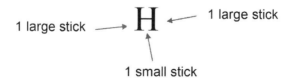

1 large stick ⟶ **H** ⟵ 1 large stick

1 small stick

Associating Numbers and Letters with Shapes or Characters

Associating numbers and letters with shapes while learning to write was effective for my son. He was familiar with the shapes, so I showed him how to connect shapes to form letters and numbers, and even to draw. This is similar to the example given previously in this book where an *A* is part triangle with a line in the middle. Let's take this a step further and use this strategy to help kids remember bigger numbers.

The number 2 looks like a swan and the number 7 looks like a hammer. This means the number 27 is a swan running from a hammer. Let's try another one with letters. The letter *D* is made up of a line and a smile turned sideways. Therefore, a story about how to make *D* could be a strong line carrying a sideways smile to make kids in the city happy. Creating stories and sentences gives letters and numbers personalities. This helps children remember how to write them, especially if they help you create the stories.

Teach the Information to Someone Else

Teaching a topic to someone else is a great way to learn something new. You may be asking yourself how a child can do this. Simple. Your child can role-play school. There are various ways to make this fun for a child. My son has stood at his Vtech Digi Art Creative Easel learning toy and taught me how to write shapes in alphabetical order. We have also done role playing where I am a student in his class and I don't know how to write letters. He taught me by verbally explaining how he wrote each letter. Now for a parent, who already knows how to write letters, this could be a waste of time. However, there is a high level of learning being executed here. Also, your child will enjoy showing off their new skills and teaching their parents.

Maybe your child is not into playing school. Another way to do this is by playing the "Problem Game" with your child and their toys. Currently, Cory loves the cartoon *Paw Patrol*, and his favorite characters are Chase and Marshall, who are puppies. Ryder, a ten-year-old boy character from *Paw Patrol*, is the leader of the pups, and he gives them various problems to solve. These problems come to Ryder through his cellphone from community leaders such as Mayor Goodway.

In our game, I am Ryder, and my son plays one of the pups. We both create various problems for the game. My problem may be that Ben, a boy who lives in the neighborhood, wants to learn how to write his name. It is one of the pups' job to teach him. Cory will pretend he is Chase teaching Ben to write his name at the easel. You can be very creative with this game!

Make It Active

Your child may see you write, but it does not become real to them until they do it themselves. **Learning comes to life for a child when you do something with the information.** Of course, sitting at a table writing is active, but you can take it a step further by making it more physical. Go outside, collect rocks, and use them to form the alphabet and numbers.

Build a writing activity around your children's interest. For example, if your child likes cars, then have them construct letters in sand or mud with their toy vehicles. You can also create a road with tape in the form of letters and numbers. Then have your child follow the path with the cars. If you have a child that likes dolls or stuffed animals, then help them role play as a teacher teaching their dolls how to write.

One activity my son loved was our Sidewalk Game! We go outside to the blacktop near our home and write large letters and numbers with sidewalk chalk. Then I tell my son he has a certain amount of time, like twenty seconds, to find the letter *A* and trace it or run on it like he was writing it with his footsteps. So he finds *A* and runs on its left diagonal line then down the right diagonal line, and across the line in the middle. Once he learned how to write independently, then he would write the letters and numbers with sidewalk chalk, and I would run. Then we would alternate who writes and who runs.

Sleep

A lot of learning takes place while we sleep. Before we talk about sleep, let discuss how the brain works.

How the Brain Works

Our brains have millions of neurons, which are the basic working units that transmit information throughout the body to other nerve cells and muscles. The neuron is made up of a cell body, axon, and dendrites. The dendrites receive information from other neurons. This information is passed down to the cell body and on to the axon in the form of an electrical signal or shock in the dendritic spine of the next neuron.

Once the electrical signal has reached the end of the axon, the information must go across a tiny, narrow gap to another neuron. The gap is called a *synapse*. The electrical signal can then cause a spark in consecutive neurons. These signals are your thoughts.

The more often a neuron shocks the next one, the stronger the brain links that are created.

Learning something new means creating new or stronger links in your brain. When you first learn something, the brain links are weak. This means that only a few neurons are linked together, and the spark between neurons is small. However, as you practice a new idea frequently, more neurons are involved, and the synaptic links get stronger, the sparks get bigger, and the brain links get more powerful. Longer brain links can store more complex information.

The opposite can happen when the neurons don't connect. You start to lose a new concept you just learned if it is not practiced enough.

So you are probably asking yourself, what does this have to do with sleep?

Learning During Sleep

Research scientist Guany Yang studies neurons and is interested in how we learn. She wondered if neurons change when we learn something new. She found that neurons do change, and they transform the most after we learn something new and then go to sleep. The dendrite spines form synapse links with the axons of other neurons, meaning brain links become stronger as you sleep.[2]

As your child sleeps, the brain reviews what it has learned during the day like writing a new letter. The nighttime "reviews" during sleep allow the dendrite spines to become bigger in your child's brain. So make sure your child is getting enough sleep at night.

---

[2] Barbara Oakley PhD, Terrane Sejnowski, PhD. "Learning How to Learn: A Guide for Kids and Teens."

The American Academy of Pediatrics supports the American Academy of Sleep Medicine guidelines for sleep in children from infants and teens:

- Infants 4 months to 12 months should sleep 12 to 16 hours per 24 hours (including naps) on a regular basis.

- Children 1 to 2 years of age should sleep 11 to 14 hours per 24 hours (including naps) on a regular basis.

- Children 3 to 5 of age should sleep 10 to 13 hours per 24 hours (including naps) on a regular basis.

- Children 6 to 12 years of age should sleep 9 to 12 hours per 24 hours on a regular basis.

- Teenagers 13 to 18 years of age should sleep 8 to 10 hours per 24 hours on a regular basis.

Learning Techniques during the Day

The more your child is exposed to writing through play and the practice of forming letters and numbers, the more they will grow new dendrite spines and synaptic links. These links grow little by little and will get stronger. Have your child spend time learning how to write letters and numbers each day for several days, weeks, or months. During this time, your child will get multiple periods of sleep. Break the learning up into small pieces such as one letter to three letters a day. This gives them more time for new synaptic links to grow and helps the learning solidify. **Practice and sleep will make the information stick in your child's brain.**

ACTIVITIES

These activities will help your child remember how to form letters and numbers. You may use all the activities or just pick one or two.

Picture Things

1. Challenge yourself and your child to create silly pictures for each letter of the alphabet and numbers 1 through 10.

   - As your child is learning to write, encourage them to verbally describe how they are making the picture.

   - For example, while drawing the letter *A*, your child will say, "Two stick man legs with a line in the middle."

Make Up Songs

1. Create songs about how to write the letters and numbers. Use a familiar tune to a song your child already knows, like "Happy Birthday" or "Old MacDonald."

   - You may create a song for each letter or number.

   - You can also create a song to write a few letters or numbers at a time.

- Another option is to create a song to write the whole alphabet and/or numbers 1 through 10. (This will be a big task, but with repetition it can be done.)

Metaphors

1. While your child is learning to write, help them create metaphors or similarities between the letter and numbers and information with which they are familiar.

   - Remember, the sillier or weirder, the better.
   - Have the child recite the metaphor while writing.
   - It is okay to laugh!

Imagination

1. While writing with your child, ask them the following questions:

   - "What it is like to be this letter?" If they don't understand this question, ask them, "What does a particular letter look like?"
   - Encourage them to think of anything in their minds, like animals, cartoon characters, family members, friends, cars, etc.

- Enhance their explanations by adding to their answers with action verbs. For example, "*M* is a monster that moves up, down, up, down."

Associating Numbers and Letters with Shapes or Characters

1. Have shapes and your child's favorite characters available to view.

2. While writing a letter or number, ask your child which shape or combination of shapes it reminds them of.

   - While writing, you may also ask your child which character or combination of characters it reminds them of.

3. Optional: have the child create stories and silly sentences associated with the letters and numbers as they are writing.

Teach the Information to Someone Else

1. Role play with your child and have them teach you how to write letters and numbers.

2. Make it interesting by dressing up.

   - Have the child dress up like a teacher.

   - The parents can dress like students in the class.

3. You and your child can also create a short movie or video teaching stuffed animals or action figures how to write.

Make It Active

1. Have your child write letters or numbers on index cards or construction paper.

2. Create and sing a song about the alphabet and letters.

3. Once a letter or number is mentioned in the song, hold it up, move it around, and dance with it.

Sleep

1. View the guidelines for sleep by the American Academy of Pediatrics, which supports the American Academy of Sleep Medicine.

2. Ensure your child is getting enough sleep.

3. Reinforce what they have learned by doing the following:

   - Asking your child about their favorite letter or number to write.

   - Telling other family members how you are using metaphors, imagination, and association to learn how to write.

CHAPTER 3

In-Depth Learning

IN-DEPTH LEARNING

What Is In-Depth Learning?

In-depth learning is being exposed to a concept in various ways. I used three of the five senses and various learning styles to expose my son to writing. As you know, the five senses are hearing, seeing, touching, tasting, and smelling. Let's use the example of a parent wanting to teach their child to write the alphabet. A parent may do the following:

- View a chart with colorful pictures of the alphabet with the child **(sight)**.

- Write the letter *A* and draw a picture associated with it, like an apple **(sight)**.

- Read an alphabet children's book aloud to the child **(sight and hearing)**.

- Describe how to write the letter *J* while drawing it, such as saying, "Line down and then hook at the bottom" **(sight and hearing)**.

- Create a song with the child about how the letter is shaped **(hearing)**.

- Form the letters with rocks or Play-Doh **(physical/rhythmic/kinesthetic)**

- Do a scavenger hunt where the child has to find all the letters with big bellies or bubbles, like letters *B, P, d,* and *b* (**physical/rhythmic/kinesthetic**).

How to Make In-Depth Learning Fun

- Do not hold long sessions with young children when trying to expose them to the writing. (Fifteen minutes of daily practice or exposure is great.)

- If the child wants to write more than fifteen minutes, then follow their lead.

- Tailor the lessons to their interests.

- Expose the child to writing in various ways through art, play, reading, toys, interaction with you, digital media, etc.

- Learn what your child's definition of fun is and incorporate this into learning.

- Play games—games incorporate all learning styles.

Learning Styles

People have several different ways they learn. These different ways are called *learning styles.* Tailoring your teaching to different learning styles is an important part of making learning fun and relaxing to children. You will learn how children with specific learning styles communicate and their favorite toys and activities to do.

Auditory Learners

Children who use **hearing** to learn are usually **auditory** learners. Below are communication methods, activities, and toys to help your child learn how to write in a fun way if he or she is an auditory learner.

Communication

- Tend to remember concepts when explained aloud
- Like to repeat aloud what they have learned
- Can retain knowledge when paired with music or clapping

Toy or Activities

- Like music
- Can remember words to songs
- Good at following spoken directions
- Like being read to
- Like wordplay and language patterns

Visual Learners

Children who use **sight** to learn are usually **visual** learners. Below are specific communication methods, activities, and toys to help your child learn new words and how to write in a fun way if he or she is a visual learner.

Communication

- Communicate through drawing and painting
- Like reading and retelling stories
- Will say, "Show me," when learning something new

Toys or Activities

- Books
- Drawing or viewing pictures
- Puzzles
- Creating storylines with sketches
- Colorful flashcards

<u>Kinesthetic/Physical (Rhythm) Learners</u>

Children who use **touch** to learn are usually **kinesthetic** learners. Below are methods, activities, and toys to help these children learn new words and how to write in a fun way.

Communication

- Learn through touch and movement
- Like to say, "Let me see that," which means, "Let me hold that."
- Like to use action words such as run, jump, play, kick

Toys or Activities

- Like building and model sets

- Enjoy interactive displays at museums

- Love to tear things apart to learn

Many young children, including my son, possess more than one learning style. Do a combination of activities from the three learning styles on the next few pages in order to help these children learn. Incorporate communication tactics and activities from all learning styles and see which one your child gravitates toward.

If you see your child struggling to grasp the concept of writing, expose them to activities that coincide with how they learn best.

ACTIVITIES

Below are writing games/activities for specific learning styles. Please note that nothing beats actually having your child sit down and practice writing. However, below are activities that will supplement writing and engrain the shape, number, and letter forms in your child's brain.

Visual Learner Writing Activities

1. Draw and paint colorful pictures of letters and numbers with your child.

2. When learning to write, "show them how" to do it.

3. Have your child watch others write on YouTube shows such as the following:

   - "How to Write Letters A–Z—Learning to Write the Alphabet for Kids—Uppercase and Lowercase Letter" by 123ABCtv

   - "Learn to Write Letters, Kids Learn Writing Alphabet A to Z, Game for Kid Android App" by Kids Games & Surprise Toys

   - "Writing Alphabet Letter for Children—Alphabet for Kids—Periwinkle" by Periwinkle

4. Get alphabet and number books with colorful pictures and have the child trace each letter and number with their finger while you are reading to them.

5. Create, take apart, and put together a puzzle with letters and numbers:

   - Make letters and numbers out of cardboard.

   - Color the letters and numbers.

   - Cut the letters and numbers into four sections.

   - Help the child put the puzzle together.

This helps with learning how letters and numbers are formed.

6. Create and illustrate stories with letters and numbers as characters.

7. Make or purchase colorful flashcards/pictures with letters and numbers. Then have the child decorate the outline of the letter with reusable stickers.

8. Have colorful word charts or boards with words for daily viewing (for example, boards with the family schedule or food menu).

   - Make the chart colorful by making one food item red and another food item green.

9. Have the child draw their interpretation of a letter or number.

    - The child who is writing the letter *Q* may draw sleepy eyes in the circular part to represent quietness.

10. Use window markers to create a story or to draw and write words in a certain category like animals or fruit.

11. Build letters that form words with blocks and a magnetic tiles playset.

12. Watch educational/literacy television shows that have letters, words, and numbers shown on the screen such as the following:

    - Super WHY!
    - LeapFrog series
    - Alphablocks (YouTube)
    - Number Blocks (YouTube)

13. Identify letters, numbers, and words while playing or running errands:

    - Read directions.
    - Read signs.
    - Read advertisements.
    - Go to museums and read new information.

14. Play a letter and number hunt game:

- Hide letters and numbers in a certain category around your home and have children find and identify them.

Auditory Learners Writing Activities

1. Listen to or watch songs based on letters and numbers, and then do the following:

- Make it fun by playing instruments while singing.

- Some books based on songs/albums are as follows:

   - *Do You Know Your Alphabet?* by Mark D. Pencil (Learning with Hip Hop album)

   - *Count to 100* by Mark D. Pencil (Learning with Hip Hop album)

   - *Learning About Numbers* by Sesame Street

   - *Alphabet Safari: A Song about Drawing with Letters (Sing and Draw!)* by Blake Hoena, Tim Palin, et al

2. Create your own recording or audiobook describing, in a silly way, how to write each letter and number.

3. Write words, letters, and numbers outside with sidewalk chalk. Give your child clues on how you wrote them and then have them run to the number or letter they think it is.

   - For example, say you are drawing a number 8.

   - A clue could be you draw a snake or letter *S* then draw a diagonal line up.

- Then tell your child to run to the number you are describing.

- The child will run to the number *8*.

- If not, give them more clues until they go to the correct number.

- Another clue could be you drew a circle on top and a circle on the bottom.

4. Make up a silly song or chant together about letters or numbers in a certain category.

    - For example, make up a song about all the numbers with straight vertical lines, like 1, 4, and 9.

    - You can also make up a song about all the lower-case letters with humps, such as *h*, *m*, *n*, and *u*.

5. Make up a bedtime story about an *A* forming himself into every letter of the alphabet.

    - For example, the story could start off like this: "Once there was the letter *A*, who wanted to be a *B*. So the Letter Shifter gave *A* two big bellies. However, *B* wanted to be the letter *C*. The Letter Shifter gave *B* a curved back and took away the two big bellies.

6. Read various books aloud, about learning to write:

    - *Dear Dragon: A Pen Pal Tale* by Josh Funk/Rodolfo Montalvo

    - *Write On, Carlos!* by Stuart J. Murphy

37

- *Little Plane Learns to Write* by Stephen Savage

- *Dear Dinosaur* by Chae Strathie/Nicola O'Byrne

7. Record a video of the child or parent identifying letters and numbers and how they are shaped around your home or outside. Play the video back so the child can hear it.

8. Play the *X* Letter and Number Game:

   - Write the alphabet and numbers 1 to 10 on large size paper, chalk board, or dry-erase board.

   - Tell the child to put an *X* around all the letters with a bubble, like *a, B, b, d, O, o, P, and p.*

   - Tell the child to put an *X* around all the numbers with a curve, like 2,3,5,6,8 and 9.

   - Tell the child to put an *X* around all the letters with a hook, like *j, g, f, and, r.*

   - Tell the child to put *X's* around various letters and numbers with different characteristics until there is an *X* on all of them.

   - Help your child if they need assistance.

9. Play bingo games where letters and numbers must be identified.

10. Spell words using a DIY puzzle.

    - Get cardstock paper and cut it into various shapes, such as circles, diagonal lines, curves, *u* shapes, *o* shapes, straight lines, hook shapes, etc.

- Name two and three-letter words, like *it, so, to, cat, pot*, etc.

- Help your child spell those words by building the letters to create them.

- For example, if the word was *so*, you should position the curvy shapes until an *s* is formed.

- Then put the *o* shape beside the *s* to make the word *so*.

11. Play a Letter and Number Identification Game (auditory style):

    - Have your child explain to you how to write a letter or number.

    - After hearing their explanation, write the letter or number they are describing.

    - You may switch with your child, where they write and you describe the letter or number.

12. Play the Adding or Subtraction Letter and Number Game

    - Tell the child you are a certain letter like *Z* but you want to add and subtract something to it to make a new letter.

    - You want to take way the top and bottom horizontal lines.

    - Then child is left with the diagonal line, */*.

    - Tell the child you want to add another diagonal line facing the opposite direction.

    - As a result, the child should make a *X*.

    - Give the child more clues until they write the correct letter.

13. Play the Same Category Game:

- Write any letter or number on paper.

- You may also get magnetic letters.

- Have the child put letter and numbers in the same category beside it.

- This game is open to your child's interpretation.

- For example, if you write the letter *W*, they may give you the letters *A, V, Y, M* because they all have diagonal lines in them.

- Discuss with your child the similarities they see in how the letters and numbers are formed.

Kinesthetic Learner Writing and Building Activities

The activities below will help your child learn to write by either writing, tracing, or building letters and numbers.

1. Hold, manipulate, and **trace** refrigerator letters and numbers with fingers to learn how they are formed.

2. Use the coins to form the shape of letters and numbers.

3. Do sand play with materials such as sand, measuring cups, spoons, shovels, and funnels.

   - Use the spoon to draw on the sand to make letters and numbers.

   - Use the cups and shovels to dig in the sand to form letters and numbers.

4. Go outside and collect objects in nature, such as rocks, leaves, flowers, pinecones, seeds, dirt.

   ▪ Form all these objects into various shapes, letters, and numbers.

5. Make various letters and numbers using Play-Doh, and then create a story with them.

6. Let your child use snacks like crackers and grapes to form into numbers and letters.

7. Go outside and use sidewalk chalk to write various letters and numbers.

   ▪ Announce the letters and numbers one at a time.

   ▪ After announcing the letters and numbers, call out an action, such as hop, skip, gallop, or run.

   ▪ For example, you might say, "A—jump!"

   ▪ Your child will go to *A* and trace it by jumping on its lines.

   ▪ Then repeat with other letters, numbers, and actions.

8. Have children sit on a bouncy ball, and verbally give them instructions on various directions to move in order to make letters and numbers:

   ▪ In order to do this activity, ensure they are familiar with how to write the specific letter and number you call out.

   ▪ Have the letter or number written in a place where they can see it just in case.

   ▪ Let's use the number 9 as an example.

- You will say, "Number 9, hop in a straight line down and then make a big bubble at the top of the line (on the left).

- If you have the number or letter visible, follow along with your finger as they are forming the letter with their hops on the ball.

9. Dance, clap, and snap while chanting how to write various letters, numbers, and shapes.

10. Form letters and numbers with Play-Doh or rocks and have your child identify it with a blind fold on or with their eyes closed.

   - If you form the number 8 with rocks, have your child feel and touch how the rocks are formed and identify the number.

   - Give your child clues if they are having trouble.

   - Keep doing this activity with different letters and numbers.

11. Take your child outside to play and identify objects such as flowers, trees, and sticks that look like letters and numbers.

   - Take it a step further by bringing pencils and a sketch pad outside to draw what you observe.

12. Have a group of children create letters and numbers with their bodies.

   - Make it fun by giving them a certain time to create the letters and numbers.

CHAPTER 4

Learning to Write Before Actually Writing

LEARNING TO WRITE BEFORE ACTUALLY WRITING

Reading Alphabet and Number Books

I started reading to Cory while I was pregnant with him. I remember watching the Dr. Ben Carson PBS Special on YouTube called *Brain Health*, where he emphasized the importance of reading to children. He also said parents should start reading to their children once babies can hear their first sounds, which is around sixteen weeks. Additionally, he said it is very important for a parent to start reading to a child once they can interact and also to discuss what is going on. This helps to build a bond between the child and the parent. It also creates connections in the brain and sets a foundation for the child to be creative and imaginative.[3]

As I was learning this new information, I became excited. When I was fifteen weeks and six days pregnant, I went to the local library and started borrowing children's books. I was so overwhelmed by the number of books to choose from and the fact that I could check out a maximum of fifty. My plan was to start with subjects I knew my child

---

[3] Dr. Ben Carson. "The Missing Link" The Science of Brain Health. PBS. https://www.ket.org/series/MLSB/all/. Accessed 4/23/2019.

would need to learn, such being kind, sharing, manners, the alphabet, shapes, numbers, and colors. I checked out ten children's books that day and started reading to Cory every night before I went to bed.

As you can see, my son was exposed to a lot of words once he was born. When I brought him home our bonding activities included me holding, touching, and looking at him and talking, playing, and reading to him. In my stack of borrowed books, I always had topics addressing the alphabet, shapes, numbers, and colors. Cory was fixated on the colorful images in the stories. Seeing the alphabet and numbers in different books written from different authors' perspectives made him very familiar with how they looked and their formation.

He began identifying letters and numbers around nine months. I remember asking him to give me the book *Thank You God* by Kathleen Bostrom in the play area book bin. He came back with the correct book. This made me realize that he may be able to identify letters and numbers. I remember drawing the alphabet and asking him to find certain letters. Because he did not know how to point yet, he would take his hand and pat on the correct letter. He did the same thing when I wrote numbers.

Picture Walking

Picture walking is a learning technique you will see many kids do, especially if they can't read yet. They will scan and look briefly through the colorful pictures, headings, words, and character motions to get a general idea of what the book is about. It is like watching a preview of a movie or checking a map before going on a trip. What children are doing is organizing their thoughts and the information they are reading or viewing. Before reading a book about letters, numbers, shapes, let them do a picture walk. This will get their minds ready to receive the information. It will also to help them identify the content and improve their writing skills in the future.[4]

Singing

After a diaper change and giving my son milk, singing was my secret weapon for soothing him when he cried in the car, at home, or in the middle of the night. When my son started to cry, it sometimes became a bit stressful because I wanted to figure out what was wrong. It can be difficult to tell what is bothering them when your child does not talk. Once I solved the problem, I became relieved. Singing was also a way to soothe myself from the burst of stress I felt when trying to stop my son from crying.

I sang songs that were familiar to me and required little brain power, such as "The Alphabet Song," "The Itsy Bitsy Spider," and "Jesus Loves

---

[4] Barbara Oakley PhD, Terrane Sejnowski, PhD. "Learning How to Learn: A Guide for Kids and Teens."

Me." During my time as a play therapist, I learned that getting kids to count is a great way to manage stress, anger, and even sadness. Counting was a calming mechanism for me when I was exhausted and had to get up in the middle of the night with Cory. As a result, my son heard "The Alphabet Song" and me counting numbers numerous times.

Songs are also a way to implant ideas in a child's mind because they activate the brain's right hemisphere. They helped my son remember the letters and numbers. When we read alphabet and numbers books, I would sing the words. I would also trace the letters and numbers with my fingers so he could see that they can be drawn or written. This helped Cory become familiar with the information by hearing and seeing it simultaneously.

The ability to identify letters and numbers means he knew what they looked like. Therefore, he had a picture in his mind about how to form them even if he could not write them yet. Familiarity was the first step in Cory learning to write.

Movement

Songs are a great way for children to learn, but when you combine songs with movement, the information really sticks. Children's songs like "Head, Shoulders, Knees, and Toes" help kids learn about body parts. The reason is, motions that are meaningful hold ideas in the child's mind and produce a spark that becomes part of that memory.

My son and I loved to hear and dance to "Do You Know Your Alphabet?" by Mark D. Pencil on Pandora Toddler Radio in our home and on the car CD player. Every time we heard a different letter, we would move our arms up and down. Sometimes, we would get do-it-yourself instruments like a water bottle filled with rice or bang the bottom of an oatmeal container and dance to it. We also danced to the Mark D. Pencil "I Can Count to 100" song. We often moved our heads forward and backward when a different number was called in this song.

Another great way to move to the letters and numbers is through association. One of my favorite alphabet books is called *Animalphabet* by Julia Donaldson and Sharon King-Chai. This book associates each letter with an animal and their movements. For example, for the letters *S* and *T*, the authors ask, "Who can slither better than a rabbit? A Snake! Who can growl better than a snake? A Tiger!" My son and I did all the movements for each animal in this book. For example, we would slither on the floor like snakes and walk on our hands and feet like a tiger.

He connected the movements to the animals and the letters. We have used this same concept with many other alphabet books, such as *Dr.*

Seuss's ABC: An Amazing Alphabet Book and *Chicka Chicka Boom Boom* by Bill Martin.

We like incorporating movement with books about numbers like *Ten Black Dots* by Donald Crews and *How Many Fish?* by Caron Lee Cohen. I remember Cory and I would hop once for one dot, twice for two dots, and so on when reading *Ten Black Dots*. When reading *How Many Fish?*, we would act like we were swimming in the ocean and make the sound "blup" for the number of fish on the page we were viewing.

An important tip about movement and learning is that it's more fun when you have someone to do it with.

I love to move and dance, so my son always has a partner!

Digital Media and Exposure to Letters and Numbers

I know there are some parents out there who are digital media free, meaning they don't let their children watch television or use smartphones or tablets. **I think parents must make the best decision for their children.** However, I think digital media can be an awesome learning tool for kids if used in the right way.

It should not be the *only* way your child learns something new, but it can supplement your child's learning. Below I will discuss the American

Academy of Pediatrics' recommendations for digital media use and how it was used to help my son with learning how to write.

Suggestions from the American Academy of Pediatrics

As of 2016, the American Academy of Pediatrics recommends that children younger than eighteen months should avoid the use of screen media other than video chatting. Parents of children eighteen to twenty-four months of age who want to introduce their kids to digital media should choose high-quality programming and watch it with their children to help them understand what they are seeing.

Children two to five years should be limited to one hour per day of high-quality programs. Parents should view the program with the child and apply it to the world around them.[5]

Other Suggestions from Experts

I remember going to the local library for a series of lectures given by a woman with a PhD in early childhood education and development. Someone from the audience asked about toddlers and young children's use of tablets, smartphones, and television.

---

[5] American Academy of Pediatrics. "American Academy of Pediatric Announces New Recommendations for Children's Media Use" https://www.aap.org/en-us/about-the-aap/aap-press-room/Pages/American-Academy-of-Pediatrics-Announces-New-Recommendations-for-Childrens-Media-Use.aspx Accessed 4/23/2019.

She suggested that digital media be used as a supplement to what the child is learning. In other words, the child should not be introduced to a concept by these digital devices, but the devices can be used as reinforcement for what the child already knows.

I thought this was good advice, so I started reading books to Cory first and then let him watch the cartoon or show associated with it.

How We Use Educational Videos for Writing

Almost every night after dinner, I allow Cory to watch television. We own a smart television, which means he can access the internet on it. He loves to watch educational videos about letters and numbers for two reasons: This topic was familiar to him, so he could follow what was going on. He liked the bright colors, music, and real-word application the videos provided.

One particular YouTube video my son loved was called "ABC Song | ABC Songs for Children—13 Alphabet Songs and 26 Videos" by Cocomelon – Nursery Rhymes. This video told a story for each letter of the alphabet. For example, the letter *A* is about an ant who jumped on an apple tree branch causing the apple to fall in Adam's basket.

The video repeatedly sings the alphabet and has the letters dancing. It also shows kids how to write letters by showing images of the alphabet being drawn on the screen during songs. This video incorporates many scientific techniques of fun learning, like association, metaphors, pictures, songs, and making it active. My son watched this video multiple times and gained a lot value from this program.

Another video he liked was "ABC's by Beans-N-Frank." The video has two characters dancing and rapping about the letters. They repeatedly say the alphabet to a catchy hip-hop beat that my son loved to dance to. The letters are shown throughout the whole video, and there is a lot of color to grab a child's attention. The rap song is about the letters and the words they begin with.

Every time Beans and Frank said a different letter, we would put our hands in the air and sing. The motion of hands in the air stuck in his mind because it created a signal in his brain that a letter was being identified. This provided us with an excellent exercise after dinner. This video incorporated the memory science of association, movement, and metaphors.

Another series we love is the Leap Frog educational videos. We first learned about these through Netflix. They are also available on Amazon.com as a rental or to own. We particular like the video *Scout and Friends Numberland*. It is about Scout, who is a dog, and his friends going on an adventure to learn about numbers. Each number is a character with a different personality.

They learn by going to a magical place called Numberland where they help the numbers count and pack their luggage to go on a trip. This video has striking images where upbeat songs are used to sing numbers one through ten repeatedly. It addresses skip counting by twos, which builds a foundation for multiplication.

My son watched this show repeatedly. I still sing the tunes from the cartoon in my head. This video also incorporates the memory science of association, movement, pictures, metaphors, songs, and movements. Watching the numbers interact with one another on television helped my son learn how they are formed.

I encourage you and your child to search for ABC and number videos on platforms such as Amazon, Netflix, and YouTube and find what your child likes. Watch the videos with your child and discuss what is happening. The best videos for kids incorporate music, songs, and colorful characters. The colorful pictures of the letters and numbers will create a picture in your child's mind on how to write. Get up and dance to the music, as movement makes new information stick to your child's brain.

Seeing Me Write and Draw

One of my go-to activities to keep my son's attention during road trips, church services, or appointments was to write and draw letters and familiar words like his name and favorite animals. I remember going to church as a young girl and writing while the minister preached because I was not interested what he was talking about at the time. During this time, all the kids would get their pencils and use the church program to write notes and play tic-tac-toe, hang man, and SOS. Now our current church has a children's service where Bible stories are presented in a kid-friendly manner.

When I became a mom, my first instinct was to resort to my childhood for attention- keeping strategies when needed. I found that my son enjoyed watching me write and draw before he could write himself. At first, I would draw shapes, like circles, squares, triangles, and rectangles and identify them. He would then take his crayon, attempting to color and identify them, and scribble over my drawings. Eventually, I started to connect the shapes to make pictures, like stick men or robots and tell him stories about the drawings. Stickmen consist of simple shapes and structures, such as circles, lines, dots, and semi-circles.

One day on a long road trip, I just finished reading the alphabet and numbers book *123 versus ABC* by Mike Boldt to Cory. I wanted to make a connection to the book because we had a long drive ahead of us and I thought it would be fun. I started writing numbers and letters by using the book as a guide and retelling the story through my writing. This book is about the numbers and letters competing to be the stars of the plot. They have funny debates that involve animals and other props.

The alphabet and numbers are fighting over the same animal, such as one alligator for 1 and *A*, two bears for 2 and *B*, and three cars for 3 and *C*. At the end, the letters and numbers conclude that they are both stars and have important roles.

This activity led to Cory wanting to observe me writing letters and numbers but with a catch. He would dictate when I wrote the next item. When he could not talk, he would take his hand and tap the paper, and I knew to write a new letter or number. When he was able to speak, he would say the letter or number. Then we started writing more but in various settings, such as on his doodle pad, outside with sidewalk chalk, on the window with window markers, on notebook paper, and on craft paper taped to the floor and wall. I will give you more details about these activities later in the book.

Another great activity is to record your child's thoughts, stories, and words. One day Cory was playing with his *Paw Patrol* action figures, Chase and Marshall. He had them on the window stool looking outside. I got paper and pencil and asked him, "What do Chase and Marshall see outside?" He told me they saw cars, trees, a garden, grass, and houses. I wrote down what he said. Two of the sentences I wrote were, "Chase sees a yellow car. Marshall sees grass." Cory was thrilled to see his words on paper.

Once your child learns to write, you may have them write your thoughts down. It is best for them to start with one- or two-word phrases like "yellow sun." You may do this activity before they start writing by having them **draw their interpretation** of your thoughts or stories.

Trained Brain

As a result of all these activities, my son's brain was trained to ponder, build, create, and write letters and numbers. They created a desire in him to want to learn how to write. He would voluntarily get a writing utensil to trace and write just for fun. If you make it fun, learning to write will be inevitable!

ACTIVITIES

The activities below will encourage your child to build letters and train their brain to write them in a fun way.

Mud Shapes Letters and Numbers

1. Go outside and make mud by mixing dirt and water.

2. Gather sticks and rocks.

3. Have your child draw shapes and write letters and numbers in the mud with the sticks and rocks.

Mud Mold

1. Go outside and make mud by mixing dirt and water.

2. Have your child use their hands to form shapes, letters, and numbers with the mud.

Pipe Cleaners

1. Form shapes, letters, and numbers with pipe cleaners.

2. Make 3-D shapes, letters, and numbers by twisting a bunch of pipe cleaners together to make one item.

Spaghetti Shapes, Letters, and Numbers

1. Boil spaghetti noodles.

2. Let the spaghetti to cool after boiling.

3. Have your child make shapes, letters, and numbers with the spaghetti.

Cut Up Shoestrings or Yarn

1. Cut shoestrings or yarn at various lengths.

2. Have your child form shapes, letters, numbers, and words with the string and yarn.

3. Kids may also wrap the string and yarn around pipe cleaners for thicker letters.

Wikki Stix

1. Use the toy Wikki Stix to bend and form shapes, letters, numbers, words.

2. Create a story about letters and numbers using Wikki Stix

   - You can make 3-D characters stand, sit, and lie down with Wikki Stix.

Pretzels

1. Give your child pretzels to form letters, numbers, and shapes.

CHAPTER 5

Beginning to Write

BEGINNING TO WRITE

Stages of Writing – What the Experts Say

According to Zerotothree.org there are five stages of writing. The first stage, at fifteen months to two and a half years old, is when the child is doing random scribbling. Controlled scribbling is the second stage at two to three years old, when the child makes circles and vertical, curved, and horizontal lines. The third stage is drawing lines and patterns, at two and a half to three and a half years old. Drawing pictures of objects or people is the fourth stage at three years to five years of age. In the fifth stage, at three years to five years old, children are experimenting with letters and numbers to write on their own.[6]

Most children first learn to write once they have the strength to hold a crayon and scribble, which is at around fifteen months. When children make their first sounds, such as coos, babbles, and cries, they are making their meaningful mark in communication to others. This is what happens in writing as well: when a child begins to scribble, they are communicating.

---

[6] Zerotothree.org. "Learning to Write and Draw" https://www.zerotothree.org/resources/305-learning-to-write-and-draw. Accessed 4/24/2019.

Coos and babbles become words, like scribbles turn into controlled strokes, lines, and shapes. Eventually, the child will create letter-formed scribbles mixed with drawings, which is their attempt to communicate in print. Then you may see a child write random letters that are connected to each other with lines.

Children who are constantly exposed to writing understand that it consists of letters and words in order for their message to be understood. As a result, they develop motivation to enhance their pretend letters and words into real ones that can be understood by others.

Writing becomes a normality for children as they are exposed to more words through reading, seeing written language, and then putting it to use. One of the best ways to learn to write is to provide children with a variety of papers and writing materials. This encourages children to explore open-ended writing and drawing.[7]

What We Experienced

My son experienced his first taste of written language and art at three months when he started going to a home daycare. It consisted of three other children who were between the ages of two and three. Whenever they did an art project, my son was included. His first creation was

---

[7] Jill Frankel Hauser. *Growing Up Reading.*

putting his handprint on a coaster for my husband on Father's Day. The projects began to progress from there. Every week he would come home with various types of art projects.

Finger and Hand Painting

My daycare provider is so creative. She would have the children make turkeys, fish, rainbows, Christmas trees, eggs, etc. out of finger and hand art. While working on these projects, the children receive so many benefits. First, it is a great activity for color recognition. It gets your child started on the right track for writing because it helps to develop their fine motor skills and strengthens their finger and small hand muscles. Hand-eye coordination and control is improved and needed to place their hand on the paper to complete their artwork. Communication and language skills are developed because children were often talking to one another about their projects.

Cory finger painting at daycare.

Results of Cory's finger paint art project.

Scribbling

One day Cory, while sitting in the high chair, observed me take a red crayon to draw lines on a white sheet of paper. Then he immediately reached for the crayon and started scribbling. He scribbled all over the paper and the table. I didn't mind because the crayon was washable, so we could clean it up with a wet paper towel or cloth. Also, I had to stay close by because I didn't want him to put the crayon in his mouth. Eventually he graduated from the high chair and was able to sit at a child-sized table and chair. This is where I taught him to draw or write just on the paper and not the table. If he did draw on the table, he knew to get a wet cloth and wipe it clean.

While scribbling, Cory was experimenting with lines, loops, and various shapes. After completing his masterpiece, he would show me his work. Then I would write his name on it and put it up so everyone who walked in our home would see it. This simple action encouraged him to create more artwork because he wanted it to be displayed. Furthermore, his scribbling eventually became letters.

Writing Lines

In the five stages of writing addressed in the beginning of this chapter, the second stage was controlled scribbling. Controlled scribbling is when the child makes circles and vertical, curved, and horizontal lines. Occasionally, my daycare provider had my son practice tracing during the day. For example, she would draw different lines on paper and my son would trace them with a crayon. Simultaneously, he was doing something different but similar with me.

Circle, Circle, Dot, Dot

During the spring and summer, Cory loved being outside playing on the playground, riding his balance bike, walking to the store, and observing children outside. Sometimes, we would sit in front of our home on the concrete and draw with sidewalk chalk. Before he started writing letters, around the age of sixteen to nineteen months, we would say chants and write at the same time.

Our favorite chant was "Circle, Circle, Dot, Dot." While saying this chant, I would draw two circles and two dots. Then I would give the chalk to Cory and he would draw the circles and dots while I was chanting. The purpose of this song was to encourage him to draw various shapes and lines. It also taught him to follow directions and improved his fine motor skills. Further, it prepared him for writing because we drew various shapes and lines that formed the alphabet. "Circle, Circle, Dot, Dot" assisted in Cory writing the letters *O, i, j, a, P, d,* and *Q* because all these letters have either a curved line or dot. Other chants I created were "Diagonal, Diagonal, Straight Line, Straight Line" and "Straight Line, Straight Line, Semicircle, Semicircle."

"Diagonal, Diagonal, Straight Line, Straight Line" taught Cory to write letters and numbers like *N, X, K, W, A, H, 1, 7, and 4.* "Straight Line,

Straight Line, Semicircle, Semicircle" taught him to write the letters and numbers *c, b, j, g, p, d, 3,* and *5.*

Cory had a lot of fun with this activity for many reasons. First it was presented to him in a rhythmic manner which coincided with his enjoyment of dancing. He is very curious and loves to observe people, so being outside around neighbors, dogs, and cars was a plus. Additionally, he gained a sense of accomplishment from being able to imitate me and seeing the results of his drawing on concrete. Plus, this activity was making a strong yet enjoyable connection of writing and drawing in his brain. Last, the use of various colors in sidewalk chalk was very stimulating.

Writing Letters

I often gave Cory an open-ended opportunity to draw or write whatever he wanted by giving him various crayons and blank paper. It started as scribbles, which led to shapes and lines. Then he eventually started to write letters. These letters were wobbly-looking but were definitely recognizable. He knew how to write letters and numbers from seeing them in books, on television, on toys, from building them, and most importantly, from watching me write and describe how I was writing them. He started writing the upper-case letters first and then the lower-case letters.

Because he was exposed to the alphabet and numbers so much, he would write them in order. At this time, I did not give him lined paper because it was just an open-ended activity. I often took pictures of the letters and numbers he was writing and sent them to my immediate family, like my mom, brother, two sisters-in-law, and father-in-law. In order to encourage playful control of his writing, I got Cory the Melissa & Doug Water Wow Reusable Alphabet and Numbers pads.

The Melissa & Doug Water Wow Reusable Alphabet and Numbers pads are fun coloring board books that contain an easy-to-grasp, refillable water pen for mess-free play. Its white pages have the alphabet and numbers and simple drawings connected to them. The water pen provides vibrant colors on the page as the child is coloring, tracing, and writing on the pad. When the water dries, the colors disappear, changing the pages white again. My son enjoyed coloring and tracing the letters. It was a great activity while waiting at restaurants and doctor offices, and during long trips.

Reading

When Cory is learning something new, one of my first actions is to find a book on the subject. In my book *Teach Your Toddler to Read through Play* I discuss how my son loves to read and how it is used to introduce him to new concepts. When he first started writing, I went to our local library and borrowed children's books on characters either learning how to write or crafting stories.

Reading books is effective because my son likes to identify with characters in books. He often becomes excited when he and a character share the same experiences. For example, Cory saw parallels between himself and the main character in the book *Write on, Carlos!* by Stuart Murphy. This book takes the reader through the process of Carlos the bunny learning how to write his name. His mom and friends help him along the way. After reading this story, Cory said to me, "I can write my name like Carlos!" I encourage you to provide your children with the same experience as they are learning to write. Below is a list of books to help you:

1. *Write on, Carlos!* by Stuart Murphy
2. *Little Plane Learns to Write* by Stephen Savage
3. *Phoebe Sounds It Out* by Julie Zwillich
4. *Ayobami and the Names of the Animals* by Pilar Avila
5. *Pinkalicious: Story Time* by Victoria Kann
6. *A Squiggly Story* by Andrew Larsen
7. *Poppy's Best Paper* by Susan Eaddy
8. *Imagination According to Humphrey* by Betty Birney
9. *Libby the Story-Writing Fairy* by Daisy Meadows
10. *The Little "Read" Hen* by Dianne de Las Casas

11. *The Day the Crayons Quit* by Drew Daywalt

12. *Little Red Writing* by Joan Holub

13. *The Obstinate Pen* by Frank Dormer

14. *Ralph Tells a Story* by Abby Hanlon

15. *You Can Write Excellent Reports* by Jan Fields

16. *Reading to Peanut* by Leda Schubert

17. *I Wanna New Room* by Karen Kaufman

18. *Word Builder* by Ann Whitford

19. *Sincerely Yours: Writing Your Own Letter* by Nancy Loewen

20. *The Best Story* by Eileen Spinelli

21. *Stink and the Incredible Super-Galactic Jawbreaker* by Megan McDonald

22. *Sequoyah: the Cherokee Man Who Gave his People Writing* by James Rumford

23. *Corduroy Writes a Letter* by Alison Inches

24. *My Duck* by Tanya Linch

25. *From Pictures to Words: A Book about Making a Book* by Janet Stevens

26. *Messages in the Mailbox: How to Write a Letter* by Loreen Leedy

27. *Yoko Writes Her Name* by Rosemary Wells

ACTIVITIES

The activities below will help you to promote writing to your child. If children have an open-ended space to create art and write, they will navigate through the five stages of writing smoothly.

Provide Various Writing Opportunities

- Give children many experiences in holding a pencil, marker, or crayon.

- Offer your child blank, unlined paper and encourage them to experiment, unless your child is an experienced writer or requests lined paper.

- Erasable doodle pads are great toys to encourage children to write.

Provide the Appropriate Materials

- Start your baby with crayons and paper at the high chair. (Supervise them in case they want to eat crayons.)

- A great tool for young writers is a marking pen because little pressure is needed to write.

- However, let your child use what is most comfortable.

- A thick children's pencil is too big for small hands.

- Set up a space for your young writer filled with writing supplies like stationery, crayons, erasers, pencils, markers, stickers, and rubber stamps.

- Let your child be creative and make a masterpiece.

Make Writing an Important Part of Life

- Have your child observe you writing grocery and to-do lists, letters, and the dinner menu.

- Have your child create signs and artwork around the house for nap time, play time, and dinner time.

- Do restaurant pretend play with your child where they are a waiter writing your order. They can also be a police officer writing traffic tickets.

- If your child can't write yet, have them draw the food items or traffic tickets.

Encourage Drawing

- Art is a way that children record their ideas.

- When your child draws, write labels and captions for their drawing if they request it.

- These labels and captions can become words they will trace or guides to shape letters in the future.

Be an Audience for Your Child's Writing

- Ask your child to read to you what they have written.

- If your child cannot read or write, have them tell you what they have drawn.

- Ask your child questions about what they have written or drawn.

- Treat their work as valid communication.

CHAPTER 6

Play with Writing

PLAY WITH WRITING

Playing with Letters and Numbers

This chapter will discuss how my son and I played with letters and numbers. We used various toys and techniques to build them, to create words, and to make simple mathematical equations. This was effective in embedding letter and number formation in my son's brain.

Play-Doh

Play-Doh is one of our favorite toys to play with because it encourages creativity and it is a great sensory toy. Before my son could form sentences, we sat together on a "play blanket" placed on the floor to make letters and numbers. I started doing this when Cory just turned one. He could identify the alphabet and numbers in books, so I wanted to build on this skill. His face lit up the first time I took three long rolls of Playdoh and made the letter *A*.

He was not speaking in full sentences at the time, so he would point to the Play-Doh to signal me to make another letter or number.

We first started with *A* through *D*, and then eventually, as time went on, we made all twenty-six letters in one play period. We also made numbers and lower-case letters. Manipulating the Play-Doh and making letters and numbers ourselves helped teach Cory how to build the letters from scratch.

Play-Doh has alphabet and number templates, but I purposely did not purchase them because I wanted my son to learn that he could take straight and curved lines to make any letter, shape, or number he wanted.

Family members did buy letters and number templates for my son. He liked to imprint them in the Play-Doh, but it wasn't until he could make the alphabet himself that he played with these.

Magnetic Tiles

Cory received Magnetic Tiles for Christmas one year. This is a science, technology, engineering, and mathematics (STEM) toy consisting of squares, triangles, and hexagons, that encourage children to build various objects by connecting the tiles together. The tiles we own contain a booklet that instructs kids on how to make towers, cars, Ferris wheels, and more. When I first showed my son this toy, he was amazed at how he was able to connect them to make various shapes.

We started out using the Magnetic Tiles to make squares, triangles, diamonds, hexagons, octagons, lines, etc. In making these shapes, I would point out if something resembled a letter or number. For example, if we made a "circular square," then I would say, "That looks like the letter O!" If we made a vertical line of squares (several squares attached to each other going in a vertical line), I would ask my son what it looked like. He would say either the number *1* or lowercase *l*. Then I suggested putting another line of squares, horizontal this time, across the top to make the letter *T*. His response would be, "Oh yeah, that's *T* !" and then we would build another letter.

Eventually we started making letters and numbers. Then we started making more sophisticated structures like robots, cars, and various characters.

Cory and I made the letter B with Magnetic Tiles.

Magnetic Letters and Numbers

Besides Play-Doh, I think my son was most interested in magnetic letters and numbers because they stuck to the refrigerator door. At one year old, I remember him getting paper from his play table and trying to stick that on the wall. He tried to do this about three times before he realized it was not going to work. Instead of telling him it would not work, I let him experiment with his hypothesis. It was a great exercise in trial and error.

When he received magnetic letters and numbers, he knew how to identify them. So, he moved on to building two- and three-letter words with his knowledge of phonics. One day he was spelling the word *mad*, and I saw him get the *m*, *a*, and *p*. However, instead of putting the *p* after *m* and *a*, he turned the *p* upside down and made it into a *d*. Then he looked at me and said, "Mad." I congratulated him on his ability to spell and then realized that he was beginning to understand how to construct words.

We would play a game called Hide and Seek Letters and Numbers which consisted of my son and I hiding letters and numbers around a room and trying to find them. Cory would be so excited when it was my turn to find the letters he hid. However, due to his excitement, he often told me where the letters and numbers were before I found them.

Sometimes after finding letters and numbers, we would identify them to each other. Occasionally, I would pretend that I didn't know a letter or number, and he would help me name it. This was a fun game that involved physical activity. Once my son became familiar with the game, we would incorporate a timer to see if we could find the letters and numbers before the buzzer went off.

Flexi Rods

Flexi Rods are not toys, but I turned them into something my son could play and learn with. These are rollers that bend to make beautiful curls in women's hair. I had four packs in my closet that I intended to use but never did. When Cory was a baby, he loved to squirm during diaper changes. I tried to give him toys like Magnetic Tiles or small stuffed animals to keep his hands busy. It wasn't until he was ten months that I gave him a red Flexi Rod. I showed him how to bend it and make various shapes. He immediately took it and started to play with it.

As Cory got older, we started using the Flexi Rods to create letters and numbers. We would put them in alphabetical and numerical order. Then we used the letters and numbers to create words and simple addition and subtraction equations.

There were several benefits to doing this activity. One is that my son learned to form letters and numbers independently. He had to be creative to form letters like *X* and *K* because it involved twisting Flexi Rods around each other and making them stand up and stick out. It also strengthened his hand, which prepared him to hold a writing utensil and have control to write.

During one of my son's wellness checkups, my pediatrician, Dr. T, saw Cory bending and twisting two Flexi Rods together. He looked and said, "What type of toy is that?" I told him it was a roller that women put in their hair but Cory liked to play with it. Dr. T said the roller was a great hand strengthener and good for fine motor skills such as the synchronization of hands and fingers. After that appointment, I figured I was on the right track with Flexi Rods.

Cory made the letters A and B with Flexi Rods and put them on my computer.

Gears

Gears are STEM toys that introduce a child to the world of building and construction. It consists of plastic gears, a crank, connectors, and interlocking base plates to make 3-D creations. It is also good for hand-eye coordination and handwriting muscles. My brother and sister-in-law gave this toy to my son as a birthday present. I remember taking this toy out of the package and playing with it before I gave it to my son.

Cory liked the fact that the colorful gears turn and you could build with it horizontally or vertically. The first thing we built was a turning platform that we could spin his magnetic letters on. Then he started building tall towers of letters and numbers. While building his structures, he would put the gears on his tower to make it move and turn. The sight of all the gears turning in the form of a letter *P* and number 12 was amazing.

In order to build with gears, a child must be strong enough to connect all the pieces that come with it. Cory had to build up the strength, but with his determination to create his masterpieces, he learned eventually. I was also there to assist him until he could play with this toy independently.

Cory made the letter P with his gear toy.

Mega Bloks/Legos

Legos and building blocks have been a long-time favorite of childhood play. The first set of blocks I got for Cory was the Mega Bloks when he was a one year old. Mega Bloks are the blocks that kids can play with before Legos. When he first got them, I would take two Mega Bloks, put them together, and pull them apart while repeating the words "together and apart." The purpose of this was to expose him to new vocabulary words and to show him that he could attach and detach them.

Cory started putting together two blocks, then three blocks, and so on. I would play beside him by making my own tall towers and robots. Then one day I spelled his name by building each letter and placing them beside one another. He was so excited about this. He said, "Mommy." I assumed from his comment that he wanted me to spell *mommy*. I completed the task, and he picked up every letter to study it. Then it became a tradition to build letters along with other structures.

We also built numbers. Our favorite activity was to build number cities with Legos and do pretend play. We would build each number from one to ten and place them beside each other. It was Lego Cat's mission to destroy the numbers. However, my son played a superhero, in which he attempted to stop Lego Cat from destroying the city.

Then we progressed to building multiple number cities. For example, we would build a city with multiples of 3, which meant we created numbers 3, 6, 9, 12, and 15 out of Legos. The protagonist in our story would be the Lego Excavator Vehicle (yes, we would actually use the term *excavator* during our play). The excavator would try to knock over and destroy the city. This time, Cory was controlling the excavator, and I was the superhero trying to save the city.

There was so much imagination and creativity used in this time of play. Building letters and numbers with Mega Bloks and Legos caused my son to think abstractly. Sometimes the letters and numbers did not look like the real thing. For example, it was difficult to build the *X* in its exact form. However, if you used your imagination and looked closely, it resembled *X*.

Cory made a Lego city with multiples of three. Pictured here are numbers 3, 6, 9, 12, and 15.

Searching for Letters in the Outside World

Cory and I like when the weather is warm because we can go outside! On the weekends, we often go out twice a day if time permits. There is so much to see outside, from bugs and plants to other children. If you are observant, you will find the alphabet and numbers formed in nature. There are plenty of places to find them, like on the playground, trees, flowers, and animals and in water.

My son is much better at making these observations than I am because he is constantly building structures that have trained his brain to think creatively. As we approached the swings on the playground, he told me the poles holding the swings up look like the letter *A*. While throwing rocks in the pond, he said the ripples reminded him of the letter *O*. Other examples are trees resembling *T*, birds shaped like the number 2, and a caterpillar beside a turtle that looks like the number 10.

To make this activity more fun, bring a camera to take pictures of your findings. You may also take a notepad and writing utensil to draw what you observe.

Pom-Poms

Pom-poms can be used to make various handicrafts, such as necklaces, garlands, and pendants, and for decorating in general. I originally purchased them to stick on self- adhesive contact paper as an open-ended art project. My son would make funny faces and shapes, and even form letters and numbers with them.

One day he dumped the pom-poms on the floor, and at first, I was a little annoyed because it was a big mess. However, instead of reacting in an angry manner, I got on the floor with him and started to make shapes with him. Afterward, we started to form the alphabet and numbers in numerical order and created the Blow Away Game. The object of this game was to blow, with our mouths, the letters and numbers we just formed until they were unrecognizable. It was a fun activity and gave Cory more exposure to letter and number formation.

Write According to Child's Interest

One of the best ways parents can teach their child new skills is to be a **learning analyst.** This means to observe your child and see where their interests lie. Watch how your child learns, and think and draw conclusions of what works and what does not. One way to execute this is to record what your child plays with and how they are learning during the day. Are they playing with dolls, blocks, cars, or household items? Are they touching, listening, and/or taking things apart? Ask yourself these additional questions: How did the learning go? What went well? What needs to be improved? How long did your child learn, play, or explore that particular concept or item?

Your job is to look for patterns. Once you have answered all the questions, draw conclusions and create activities centered around them. For instance, my neighbor's child loves to dance. She will play music and move all day if allowed. Use this as an opportunity to use dance as a way to enhance the child's letter and number formation skills.

A great writing activity for this child is to make letters and numbers using body movements. This means the child is writing in the air with their arms. In order to make a *P*, the child would draw a straight line by starting from her head and moving her body to the ground. Then she would make the curved lined by standing up and drawing a curve or semicircle. A parent could also get siblings or friends involved. Both children can lie on the ground and make letters and numbers with their bodies.

If you have a child who loves basketball, then go outside and draw large letters and numbers with sidewalk chalk. Next have the child dribble the basketball around the outline of the letters and numbers. You can also have the child draw a letter or number every time they attempt a shot. The sky is the limit with being creative according to your child's interest.

Interleaving

Interleaving is practicing different techniques and aspects of the skill that is being learned. When a child is in school learning a particular topic, the teacher usually assigns problems on that subject. Many times, teachers are using textbooks as a guide to relay information to children. However, interleaving is difficult for textbook writers to do because there is usually a need for questions at the end of the chapter or unit that focuses on that chapter topic. This means, the parents may have to do the interleaving themselves.[8]

Let's discuss how to use this when learning to write. As mentioned earlier, part of learning to write is for the child to scribble, strengthen hand muscles, create art, trace, learning letter and number formation, etc. One day, instead of having the child just practice writing letters, how about adding a hand-strengthening activity like spraying a water bottle, crumbling paper, squeezing sponges, or playing with Play-Doh? On another day, you could have your child trace letters and numbers on a big sheet of paper by finger painting or have them build them using Legos.

Your child is learning to write in different ways, and it causes the brain to make deeper connections. This is ultimately **fun in-depth learning.**

---

[8] Barbara Oakley PhD, Terrane Sejnowski, PhD. "Learning How to Learn: A Guide for Kids and Teens.

ACTIVITIES

The activities below will strengthen hand-eye coordination and fine motor skills needed for writing. They will also encourage kids to play with writing and provide them with the skills needed to do it well.

Tracing Various Items

- Give your child tools such as magnetic letters and numbers, cookie cutters, cups, jars, and small books and have them trace the items on paper.

Transferring Items

- Give your child tongs or tweezers and have them transfer poms-poms, beans, and cotton balls from one bowl to another bowl.
- Your child can also transfer water from one bowl to another bowl by filling an eye dropper with water and squeezing it out.

Cutting

- Have your child practice cutting by giving them pages from old magazines.
- Then have your child cut lines and shapes you have made.
- Once they have mastered this, draw bubble letters and numbers for your child.

- Then have them cut the numbers and letters.

Cheerio, Macaroni, and Bead Necklaces

- Let your child string or put Cheerios, macaroni beads, and cut-up straws on a string to make a necklace.

- Help the child make at least three necklaces.

- After they have completed the task, tie the two string ends in a knot.

- Help the child form the necklaces into various shapes, letters, and numbers.

Cooking with Letters and Numbers

- Help your child make letters and numbers with cookie dough.

- Bake the dough in the oven and eat the letters and numbers.

Other Activities to Strengthen Fine Motor Skills Are Playing with the Following:

- Pop Beads

- Pop Tubes

- K'Nex

- Pegboards for Kids

- Small Legos

CHAPTER 7

Starting to Write Independently

STARTING TO WRITE INDEPENDENTLY

Tracing My Letters and Numbers

Cory always loved the fact that with a stroke of a crayon or marker on paper, he could create a picture. He learned this because he frequently observed me writing and drawing. One of the first things I wrote, during his observations, was the alphabet and numbers. I strategically wrote this because he would see them in books all the time. I wanted to make connections in his brain and spark his interest because it was something he was familiar with. After observing me write, he wanted to try it himself.

He started by tracing my letters and numbers. To keep it interesting, he used a variety of objects, besides crayons and markers, to trace. One of his favorite activities was to paint over letters that I drew. He also would dip his hands in paint and outline the numbers I drew on large craft paper. Another activity he liked was taking stickers or small pieces of paper to cover letters and numbers my daycare provider wrote. Tracing helps tremendously with teaching kids about the formation of letters and numbers. Sometimes doing it with just writing utensils can be monotonous for kids. Make it fun by using different craft and toys to trace.

Cory putting small pieces of paper on the outlines of the letters r, b, and o.

Tracing Name

My son often did art projects at daycare and at home on the weekends. Art is great because it inspires kids to be creative and to use their imaginations. It is the number one activity that requires kids to think outside the box, and it encourages them to be themselves.

Art is also a great way to make writing fun and appealing to young kids. Children are naturally drawn to art, so why not use it to learn other subjects such as writing?

After completing an art project, I would write Cory's name on his creations. Before writing independently, he liked to trace his name. He started by tracing the first few letters, and then he was able to complete his entire name with a crayon. One time we went outside and collected sticks. Then I broke the sticks in small pieces and wrote his name with large letters on a big sheet of paper. Then we glued the sticks on the letters so it outlined his name.

Another time I let him rip pages from old magazines and we formed the paper to spell his name. However, his favorite activity was to trace his name with paint and a paintbrush and then make various shapes in the background.

Tracing with Melissa & Doug Alphabet and Numbers Placemats

Once my mom saw that Cory could trace and write wobbly letters independently on paper and with the Melissa & Doug Water Wow pad, she gifted him the Melissa & Doug Alphabet and Numbers Placemats. The alphabet mat has traceable letters on a wipe-on-and-off surface. It also has space where the child can write their letters independently. The numbers mat has numbers 1–100 as well as 1,000, 10,000, 100,000, and 1,000,000 on it with a space where kids can write their own numbers. I gave Cory washable markers to use on the mat. This worked well because it was easily cleaned with a wet cloth.

My mother got this mat for Cory when he was two years old. I originally thought it was too advanced for him. However, I showed Cory how to trace the letters because he may like it. He was excited to give it a try after my demonstration and he started tracing right away.

These mats kept him busy while I was cooking, washing and folding clothes, and cleaning. I could see that he liked and had a determination to learn how to write. This ended up being one of the best tools to hone my son's writing skills.

Tracing letters on the Melissa & Doug Handwriting Mat while eating a snack.

Starting with Capital Letters

Cory developed a desire to write because he was always exposed to letters and numbers through reading, playing, and watching digital media. He especially liked walking to the playground and recognizing letters and numbers on car license plates. He also liked identifying them on signs and advertisements while running errands with me.

As mentioned earlier, he wrote his first letter *A* at twenty-one months. From this time on, he was determined to write all the uppercase letters. Cory often asked me for paper and writing utensils such as crayons and markers to practice. Writing is what kept his attention when I was on the telephone or during wait times in the car and community.

Cory remembered how to write the letters because I used the memory science techniques discussed in chapter 2. When Cory started writing independently, he was very verbal. When writing the letter *R*, he would say, "Line down, curve, and line out." When writing the number 7, he would say, "Line across and line down." As soon as he learned how to write the letters and numbers, he slowly became less verbal when writing because their formations were now imprinted in his brain.

As time went on, his capital letter formation mirrored a child's who had been writing for a while independently. Then I encouraged him to write lowercase letters.

Moving on to Lowercase Letters

I didn't want to push Cory to write lowercase letters because he was an early writer. My goal was to have him enjoy the process of learning. The way I encouraged him to write lowercase letters was to model it. For example, if we were writing on the window with window markers, he would write the uppercase letters and I wrote the lowercase letters. As time progressed, he wanted to write the lowercase letters like me. If he forgot how to write a letter, then I would write it and use one of the scientific learning techniques, *imagination*, *metaphor*, or, *association* to describe how I did it. There were times when I would not write it and just describe how to it. This helped him remember what to do.

Building Sentences

After he learned to write the lowercase letters, we began to write words and then sentences. I wanted Cory to have a connection to what we wrote, so we would retell various stories with words and sentences. Cory and I would alternate writing words until we created a full sentence. One sentence we wrote came from the popular story, "The Three Little Pigs," which said, "The wolf huffed and puffed and blew the house down."

My son loves to laugh, so we also wrote silly sentences. Cory was amazed to learn that there was an animal that sprayed a stinky liquid to scare away potential predators, called a *skunk*. I remember he laughed so hard when he found this out. To this day, when he sees a picture of a skunk, he laughs and makes a big deal out of it. One sentence we wrote was, "The skunk sprayed the kids and make them stinky." This made writing fun and entertaining for him.

Writing sentences during this time served a number of purposes. Cory learned how to write using uppercase and lowercase letters simultaneously. He was also introduced to grammar and how to properly communicate a written thought. His brain had to work a little harder to switch between the two sizes of letters. Last he learned to model the types of sentences we often saw in the books we read.

Learning to Write Numbers

Cory learned to write uppercase letters and numbers at the same time. He often chose what he wanted to write. I did not force him to work on letters for a certain period and then numbers or vice versa. I was aware that he had a desire to write and draw, so I did not push the issue. I think it was because he was exposed to letters and numbers simultaneously so he figured he should learn to write them together.

Many of the shapes used in writing numbers apply to letters. Also, learning to write numbers is a shorter process because 0–9 are all that need to be learned. Once Cory learned this, he was excited to start writing numbers 10–100. When he was two years old, he took pride in writing numbers 1–100 independently.

Making Mistakes

I believe failing and making mistakes is one of the most important aspects of learning anything. My goal was to instill this belief in my son. However, like many children, he gets frustrated when he can't do something. I tried to make light of these situations by telling him, "Good job trying," or, "Keep trying," or telling him to take a break.

One other phrase I used when he became irritated about a mistake was, "Your brain is stretching!"

Powerful Children's Book about Making Mistakes

I adopted this phrase from the children's book, *Your Fantastic Elastic Brain, Stretch It, Shape It* by JoAnn Deak, PhD. This book uses a diverse group of young characters to educate its reader on the powerful brain. A few concepts addressed in this book are parts of the brain and their functions. My son and I learned that the **amygdala controls your emotions, and the hippocampus helps you store and find memories**. It also teaches that the **first ten years of life is when you train your brain to grow faster.**

I was thrilled when we read the fact, **"Making mistakes is one of the best ways your brain learns and grows."** Many children get frustrated when they are learning something new, because mistakes are made, which is part of the process. This book has taught me one way to handle my son's frustration as he experiences the trial-and-error process. I am able to remind my son that his brain is growing when there is a misstep. As a result, his frustration usually decreases, and his focus on the task increases.

Dr. Deak encourages the risk of being wrong in order to stretch the brain. After reading the book, I would give my son practical examples of how mistakes lead to great inventions. Many times, after flipping on the light, I would tell Cory that it was invented by Thomas Edison, and he made ten thousand mistakes before making it.

I also told him about my failures. He had always been amazed that there was a time when I was unable blow up a balloon. There were many times he tried in the past and failed. I told Cory that I tried and tried many times to blow up a balloon since I was five; however, it didn't happen until I was eight years old. My son heard this story and kept trying to blow up a balloon since he was three. Now he is able to blow up a balloon as a four-year-old because he kept trying.

Offer more encouragement when your child **makes the effort** to write. This praises their effort and motivates them to try again until they learn a new skill. When they get frustrated, remind them that their brain needs them to keep at it until it makes a strong connection with the new learned skill. As mentioned before, the doodle pad, with its quick erasing abilities, encouraged my son to make mistakes when writing.

ACTIVITIES

The activities below will encourage your child to write by using fun methods that are appealing to children.

Write Letters and Numbers with Household Items Such as...

- Whipped cream
- Shaving cream
- Rice in a bin that you can draw letters and numbers in with fingers
- Finger paint
- Toothpaste
- A foggy window

Write Letters and Numbers in a Tray with Finger

- Fill a tray with kinetic sand and write.
- Fill a tray with cornmeal and write.
- Fill a tray with oatmeal and write.
- Fill a tray with mud and write.
- Mix one cup each of cornstarch and water and let it sit for ten minutes to make a paste. Then dip a thin paintbrush in drops of food coloring and have the child write on the paste.

Form Letters and Numbers on the Body

- Write letters and numbers with your finger on your child's hand, arm, and leg and see if they can guess what you wrote.
- Let your child write with their finger on your hand, arm, and leg and guess what they wrote.
- Put lotion on your child's arm or leg and write on the lotion

Art with Cardstock Paper or Cardboard

- Write letters and numbers on cardstock paper or cardboard.
- Let your child trace the letters or numbers with glue.
- Then put glitter, rice, or oatmeal on the glue.
- As a result, your child will have textured letters and numbers to feel.

Make 3-D Paint Letters and Numbers with Your Child

- Mix two tablespoons of each the following items together: flour, salt, and water.
- Add two drops of food coloring to the mixture. This makes puffy paint.
- Pour mixture into a squeeze bottle.
- Have the child draw and trace shapes, lines, letters, and numbers on cardboard.

CHAPTER 8

Learning in Different Settings

LEARNING IN DIFFERENT SETTINGS

Before we discuss learning in different settings, let's talk about working memory.

Working Memory

A person's working memory, which is above the eyes in the prefrontal cortex, helps them retain information. It deals with the current information you have in your mind. For example, if you are introduced to someone and they tell you their name, the working memory helps you remember it. However, sometimes information can slip your mind if you are not focusing on memorizing it. Let's say a person tells you their name, and you are thinking about your response in the conversation; then you will probably forget their name. So if you ever forget information after you just heard it, that means you probably were not focusing on it.

The Importance of Learning in Different Settings

It is effective to learn new things in different settings because your working memory senses things while you are learning. For example, when your child is learning to form letters and numbers, the working memory is helping them understand the topic, but it also notices the feel, smell, and look of the learning environment. If your child is always writing at the dining room table, then the working memory becomes accustomed to it. When your child's long-term memory is pulling out how to form letters and numbers, the brain links the kitchen table to this information.

If your child is always writing at the kitchen table but takes a written test in the classroom, their working memory may get slightly confused. The working memory will have to work harder in finding the writing information links, which may cause them to do worse on a test. A better solution would be to write in a variety of places.

Sometimes schools don't give children this variety, but it can definitely be done at home. Maybe on Mondays, writing is done at the kitchen table and on Tuesdays, it is done in their room. On Wednesdays, you could do it outside on a park bench or on the sidewalk with chalk. Writing in various settings can be in different rooms within your home or in different facilities.

Next, we will discuss how we took this concept to another level with not only writing in different settings but also using various canvases and supplies.

Sidewalk Chalk

I will not say a lot about this because it was addressed in previous chapters. However, sidewalk chalk is one of my son's favorite writing utensils. It makes the writing process social, creative, and fun. Whenever we go outside, sidewalk chalk, along with bubbles, is something I always bring with me. There have been numerous times when we played outside and my son asked for the sidewalk chalk to draw or write with other kids. He can choose from various colors to make his creations. Also, his masterpiece stays on the ground until it rains, so others who walk by can admire it.

I remember one day, on our way to the playground, he saw older kids playing on one side of the basketball court. He said, "Mommy, let's go over there!" He saw one boy his age who could not keep up with the older kids. My son started drawing with the chalk, and the little boy came over. We were able to give him chalk, and they drew pictures together. The boy's mom was very thankful.

We have also made pit stops at the same blacktop to write stories. The other day, my son and I wrote a short story about a skunk who sprayed kids with his stinky liquid. I wrote one sentence then he wrote the next. The first two sentences of the story went like this, "Once there was a skunk. He wanted to play on the playground." My son spelled playground incorrectly, but when I corrected him, he was very receptive. It was because he wanted to get his story right, and this activity was fun simply because we were outside.

On the Window

I first learned about window markers on Pinterest. After witnessing a child writing and drawing on the window, I thought to myself, "Every child would enjoy this activity!" Immediately, I went online and ordered one pack of window markers. My son was a one- year-old at the time when I demonstrated how to use them by drawing shapes and writing letters and numbers. Then as time went on, he took over and started drawing and writing himself. He especially enjoyed using the spray bottle to squirt the water and clean the window. It was an easy way for him to erase and draw something else.

A benefit of window markers is that they can be used on rainy days and during cold weather. On cold days, we usually set up the space heater to keep us warm as we create art. Writing on windows usually requires a child to stand up and write, which is called "working on a vertical surface." According to TheInspiredTreehouse.com, there are several benefits to this:

- It promotes **shoulder/elbow stability**, which allows children to use bigger movement to encourage strength and flexibility throughout the joints and muscles of the upper extremities.

- It improves **bilateral coordination,** which is the ability to use both sides of the body simultaneously in a controlled manner. This is helpful when a child tries to trace an object. They need one hand to write and the other hand to hold the paper or template.

- Midline crossing is the ability to reach across the middle of the body with arms and legs to the opposite side. This allows your child's dominant hand to get practice to develop fine motor skills. If not, then both hands will get equal practice in developing skills and the revelation of your child's dominant hand may be delayed.

- Writing on a vertical surface puts the wrist in an extended position and encourages hand stabilization for better control of the writing utensil and pencil grasp.

- Directional terms such as up, down, left, and right are easier to understand because they can be drawn in relation the child's body.

- It also helps a child develop core strength and posture by helping them maintain an upright posture.

Other ways to have your child write on a vertical surface is on a dry-erase board and chalk board.

Drawing and writing on a vertical surface

Dry-Erase Board

We have a dry-erase board in our kitchen. We use it to write the day's menu and also important facts. Before Cory started writing, he always observed me writing on the dry-erase board before eating. He understood that what I wrote pertained to eating. I remember one day I wrote *avacado* on the dry-erase board, and he told me it was spelled wrong. I had a "brain fart" that day and spelled it wrong. He told me to put an *o* in between the *v* and *c*. It turns out he was correct. This shows that he was paying attention to what he was eating and its spelling.

Now that he writes independently, it is his job to write the menu. This task has helped him learned to spell various words in the food and drink category, such as *chicken, sweet potato, blackberries, stew, soup, rice, vegetables*, *zucchini*, *avocado*, *strawberries*, etc. He also numbers the menu so he will know how many different foods he will eat.

Because my son pays attention to the dry-erase board, I record important information on it. This includes our address and phone number and Cory's full name. I wanted him to know this information in case he got lost. Because he saw it every day on the board and I review it frequently, he now knows this information without looking at the board.

Other information I will put on the board is anything new we are learning. For example, he was interested in learning how to spell the colors. As a result, I put the colors on the board, and he eventually learned how to spell and write them himself. One day, while eating a blackberry, he asked what the bumps on it were called. I did not know so I looked it up on my smartphone and found they were called *drupelets*. I wrote the word on the board, and to this day he has not forgotten it.

On Craft Paper

We have a lot of fun writing on craft paper, which can also be called *flip chart paper*. It is just a large piece of paper where children can paint, write, draw, and make art. Some people use butcher paper as an alternative. I sometimes hang it on the wall with painter's tape, and then there are times when we tape it to the floor. My son likes taking thin and medium-sized paint brushes to write letters and numbers. We have also made colorful collages of shapes, stick men, and animals with paint.

The one activity that stands out is creating a three-sentence story about an elephant who loved to play with friends. Then we used the bottom of the paper to illustrate our story. We have also glued a skeleton puzzle together on the paper and labeled the bones.

Another activity we enjoyed was drawing monsters from numbers and letters using the book *Draw AlphaBeasts* by Steve Harpster. For example, my son would write the number 2 and add on to it to draw a monster using the step-by-step instructions given in the book. This taught my son that drawing is all about combining various shapes to create an image. These types of activities will help to enhance a child's writing skills.

Notebook Paper

I remember one time forgetting to put the doodle pad in my son's bookbag on our way to a restaurant. My son was frustrated that we forgot it. Thankfully, I always keep a notebook pad and crayons in his bag just in case. This was a great alternative to the doodle pad. That day in the restaurant we learned how to play the game, Tic-Tac-Toe. The object of the game is to be the first player to make three consecutive X's or O's horizontally, vertically, or diagonally. Along with learning the strategy of the game, he was also able to practice writing O's, X's, and the lines that made up the game grid.

Of course, we have used it to write letters and numbers, but we played other games such as Stand Man. It is like the game Hang Man, but we draw the man standing instead of hanging. Stand Man is a paper-and-pencil guessing game where one player thinks of a word, phrase, or sentence and the other person(s) tries to guess it by suggesting letters or numbers within a certain number of guesses. This is a great game for teaching spelling, writing, and patience. My son has learned how to spell words such as *playground, mouse, elephant,* and *bottle* with this game.

Another great use of a notebook pad is to record findings from nature or science experiments. During the spring, fall, and summer seasons, we like to take nature walks on a trail near our home. The trail is filled with plants, flowers, trees, insects, rocks, etc. We love to go in the early spring when we can witness the life cycle of a frog. Our frequent trips allow us to see tadpoles turn into froglets and then frogs. It is beneficial to have your child draw what they see in nature and then label it. Labeling is a great writing exercise for kids because it helps to further explain their drawings. This is a fun and effective reflective activity for children. It creates a photographic memory of what they experience in nature. As soon as they look at their drawing in the future, the picture activates the brain to remember what they saw.

My son and I do a lot of science experiments because they are hands-on and satisfy his curiosity. Some of the science experiments we have done are create a rocket with balloons, string, and chairs; testing buoyancy with aluminum foil and pennies; and making food coloring float with salt in a drinking glass. Each science experiment helps us discover something new about our world.

Recording our findings with notebook paper also helps us hold on to what we learned and can be a catalyst for other experiments. For example, we wrote down that combining vinegar and baking soda creates a bubbly chemical reaction. We used this knowledge to participate in and understand another science experiment where the gas from vinegar and baking soda could be used to blow up a balloon. The experiment is called the Magic Balloon.

Cory and I doing the Magic Balloon experiment

Outside

As you know, we love going outside to write with sidewalk chalk. However, there are other ways to have fun with writing outside. One method is to paint the sidewalk with water or watercolors. This involves bringing a bucket of water and various sized paint brushes outside to draw pictures and write letters, numbers, and words. Depending on how hot it is outside, the sun may dry up your work, but this just gives your kids more opportunities to write and draw.

If it is snowing outside, you can paint the snow with a spray bottle. My son did this at daycare, and they had a great time. For this activity, fill a spray bottle with cold water (as hot water may melt the snow) and combine it with a few drops of food coloring. Then have your kids be creative and paint the snow. I have seen some kids make shapes, words, or numbers. Your kids can also create abstract artwork. If they don't form letters or numbers, it is still beneficial because spraying water bottles is a great hand strengthener for writing.

In the Bathtub

Before I had children, I didn't know bathtub crayons existed. The idea came to mind when I saw a young Cory trying to use his finger to write on the sides of the tub with water. He was disappointed when nothing would appear. So I looked online and was happy to discover that bathtub crayons do exist, and could not wait for Cory to try it. When I first showed him the crayons, he wanted to take a bath right away. That night, the sides of the bathtub were full of letters and numbers. Sometimes we play games like Tac-Tic-Toe and I would tell him where to put my *X*. This also gives him opportunities to write on a vertical surface, which we already know has multiple benefits.

Another great activity is to do finger painting in the bathtub. Bathtub finger paint was a birthday gift from my daycare provider. It is a little messy, but my son would use water to rinse it clean. After bath time, I would finish cleaning the tub with bathroom cleaner. This paint allowed my son to create pictures and label stories with words and numbers in the bathtub.

Writing in the bathtub.

ACTIVITIES

The activities below will give your child more opportunities to write and draw in different settings.

Draw My Story

- Decorate your home or a room in your home with your child's artwork so it looks like their personal art gallery.

- Tell your child a short story.

- While you are telling the story, have your child interpret the story by drawing it.

- After completing your story, have the child tell you what they have drawn.

- Now have your child tell you a story.

- It is your turn to draw their story.

- After their story, tell them about your drawing.

Library Flip

- Take a trip to the library.

- Have your child pick books of their favorite stories to read.

- Have your child create a different version of the story.

- If your child's favorite story is "The Three Little Pigs," then encourage them to change the story to something like "The Three Big Ants."

- Help your child write or draw their story.

- For example, the story could be about three big ants blowing down the wolf's house.

Record Emotion

- Children experience emotion everywhere, so this activity could be done in various places.

- Have your child record their emotion.

- Let's say they are sad because they didn't want their playdate to end.

- As you are in the car on your way home, have your child tell you why they are sad.

- Then have your child record their feelings by drawing or writing them down.

- End on a positive note by having them record or draw their favorite part of the playdate.

- They can also draw or write what they would do on their next playdate so they will have something to look forward to.

Picture Inspiration

- Show your child an image like an old family photo, famous painting, or picture from a magazine.

- Have your child draw or write anything that comes to mind about the picture.

- Ask them to write what the picture reminds them of.

- If they cannot write, have them tell you and you write it for them.

- They can also write about what it would be like if they were in the picture.

The Perfect Meal

- While your family is waiting for food at a restaurant, have your child write and/or draw their perfect meal.

- Have them write or draw how it will taste and how it will look on the plate.

- They may write or draw the colors and shapes of the food.

- Below are possible questions your child can answer in their drawing or story…

  - Do they plan to eat all their food or save some for later?

  - Will they share their food with other family members?

  - How will they feel after eating their food?

Number Inspiration

- Show your child a series of magnetic numbers, foam numbers, or numbers you have written.

- Have your child draw a picture or write a story with all the numbers as characters.

- Have your child tell you about the meaning of their story or drawing.

CHAPTER 9

Holding Writing Utensils Correctly

HOLDING WRITING UTENSILS CORRECTLY

The process of a child learning to hold a writing utensil correctly is important. I didn't pay much attention to how my son was holding crayons until my mom brought it to my attention. Then I started researching the stages and realized how accurate this information was to my experience. After doing the research, I started to model and show my son how to hold crayons and markers. Thankfully, it was not a frustrating process. It was actually very smooth because I learned the right techniques and tools to use. Below is what I found.

Stages of Writing

Many children go through four stages of holding a writing utensil. These stages guide children until they have the ability to hold the writing tool correctly.

The first stage is the *fist grip*, which is when the child holds the crayon/pencil in their whole hand like a dagger. They often use their whole arm and shoulder to move a crayon to draw and make marks.

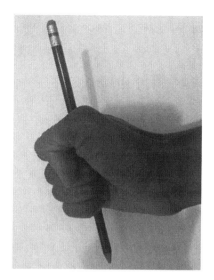

The second stage is the *palmer* or *digital pronate grasp*. Children hold the crayon/pencil with their fingers holding down the writing tool with the palm of their hand facing down toward the paper. The child's shoulder and elbow are used to scribble or draw.

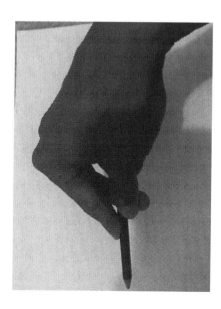

The *static tripod grip* is the third stage. At this stage the child is almost holding the pencil in the correct position but the spacing is narrower than it would be if held in a mature writing grasp. During this time, the child is writing and drawing with their wrist and with large finger movements. They are usually able to copy shapes, numbers, and letters. Furthermore, pictures of people become clearer, with arms, legs, and facial features.

The fourth stage is the *dynamic tripod* or *mature grip*. This is considered the correct hand grip where the child holds the pencil between the thumb and index finger with the pencil supported on the middle finger. The fingers are curled around the writing tool. Writing is the result of the child's finger movements.

Broken Crayons

My daycare provider sent a picture with my son writing with a broken crayon. Under the picture was a caption that said, "Broken crayons help children learn to grasp the pencil correctly." Once I read this, my first instinct was to do research. I found that occupational therapists recommend smaller crayons because they are easier for small hands to handle and manipulate.

It also discourages children from pressing too hard on the writing tool and gives them more control of what they are drawing or writing. MamaOT.com says broken crayons naturally encourage kids to pinch the crayon between their thumb and index finger, which moves them toward a more mature and skilled grasp pattern. The reason for this is it's difficult to use a palmer or digital pronate grasp on a short crayon.

My son was used to writing with broken crayons at daycare, and he would intentionally break the ones we had at home. Like many parents, I was bothered by this when I saw him doing it. So I designated one pack of crayons that could be broken, and stored away the new packs I had on hand. Many times, crayons become broken once a child uses them for a while, so I decided to keep them because of their benefit to my son's handwriting skills.

If breaking crayons bothers you, there is a product called Crayon Rocks. This product comes in multiple colors and is designed to strengthen the tripod grip muscles, preparing children for handwriting. It also helps small fingers to color in large, wide strokes while creating pictures.

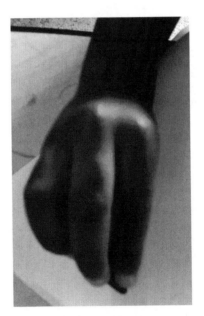

Writing with a broken crayon in hand.

Alligator Grip

I read about a strategy online called the Alligator Trick and have used it to teach my son how to hold writing utensils. It was first introduced to me by a blog post called "How to Teach a Child to Hold a Pencil Correctly" by Meeghan Mousaw. This blog is on SightandSoundReading.com. It is about a mom and kindergarten teacher who taught her little ones how to hold a pencil.

The Alligator Trick involves the following:

- Telling your child to pretend their writing hand is an alligator.
- Now they have to open and close their hand or the alligator's mouth to show that he is hungry and wants to eat the pencil.

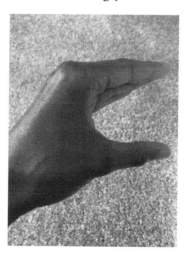

- Once the alligator is holding the pencil in his mouth, place the pencil on the bottom jaw of the alligator.
- Then close his mouth on the pencil.

- Tell the child that the alligator does not like the pencil so he puckers his lips.

- As he is puckering his lips, his jaw curls into the shape of an O.

- Then he clenches the pencil in his teeth.

Tools to Help with Writing Grasp

Some parents choose to purchase tools to assist their children with holding a writing utensil. **What has worked for us is patience, practice, broken crayons, and the Alligator trick.** If you choose to go a different route, then below are some options to consider.

I encourage you to do your research and consult reviews to determine if these tools are right for your child.

Baumgartens

Baumgartens is a twist-and-write pencil that assists kids in writing properly. It uses the right tripod finger posture to teach kids to write the correct way. It comes with dual-action erasers and extendable pencil lead.

Firesara

Firesara is a 3-D owl-design pencil-grip tool that requires children (and adults) to put their thumb and index finger into the hole on the side. It has a small tail attached that will automatically fix their ring finger, helping to teach your child the correct handwriting grasp.

The Pencil Grip

The Pencil Grip was designed by a doctor to be a one-size-fits-all product to help kids (and adults) improve handwriting. It is a training tool that adds comfort to writing. This product fits on pencils, pens, crayons, markers, paintbrushes, etc.

ACTIVITIES

The activities below help teach and improve your child's writing grasp.

Oil and Food Coloring Experiment

The use of pipettes in this experiment strengthens your child's pincer grasp, which is needed for writing.

Materials

- Vegetable oil or baby oil

- Water

- Food coloring

- Pipettes

- Cups/bowls

- A pie pan or shallow dish

Procedure:

- Fill a shallow dish with oil

- In a cup combine three to five drops of food coloring with water and mix.

- Use a separate cup for each color of water you want to make.

- Give your child pipettes and have them squirt the various colors of water into the pan of oil.

- Your child will see that water and oil do not mix.

- The results are amazing!

Oil and food coloring experiment.

Toothpicks and Grapes Activity

Grabbing grapes and putting them on toothpicks strengthens your child's pincer grasp, which is needed for writing.

Materials:

- Toothpicks

- Grapes

- Bowl

Procedure:

- Give your child a bowl of grapes and several toothpicks.

- Stay close if you are doing this activity with young children.

- Have your child create various designs by putting the grapes on the ends of toothpicks.

Building with grapes and toothpicks.

Stringing O-Shaped Cereal

Putting cereal around uncooked spaghetti noodles or toothpicks will strengthen your child's pincer grasp, which is needed for writing.

Materials

- Play-Doh or Clay

- Uncooked spaghetti noodle or toothpick

- O-shaped cereal

Procedure:

- Have your child stick an uncooked spaghetti noodle or a toothpick in a thick rounded piece of Play-Doh or clay.
- Have your child take the O-shaped cereal and string it on the spaghetti noodle or toothpick.

Sorting Coins

Picking up coins and sorting them will strengthen your child's pincer grasp, which is needed for writing. Your child may also use the coins to form letters and numbers.

Materials

- Various coins
  - Quarters, dimes, nickels, and pennies

Procedure:

- Have your child put coins that are alike in the same pile.
- Have your child compare the colors and sizes of the coins.
- Teach your child the monetary value of the coins while doing this activity.

Beaded Bracelets

Stringing beads will strengthen your child's pincer grasp, which is needed for writing.

Materials

- Various sized beads
- String

Procedure:

- Have your child string various sized beads on the string.
- Once your child has completed the task, tie both ends of the strings in a knot.

Remove the Tape

Your child will need to use the pincer grasp to peel the tape off the surface. They also need coordination and control to prevent the tape from sticking to itself.

Materials

- Masking tape
- Various color paint and paintbrush (optional)

Procedure:

- Stick various sizes (long and short strands) of masking tape to a table or flat surface
  - Choose a surface where the tape will pull off easily.
- You may add color to the tape by painting it with washable paint.

- Let the paint dry.

- Have your child peel the tape off the surface.

- Your child may stick the tape back on the surface to create art.

CHAPTER 10

What to Do When Your Child Does Not Want to Write

WHAT TO DO WHEN YOUR CHILD DOES NOT WANT TO WRITE

You may have the experience where it is writing time and your child does not want to do it. Here are some alternative activities for your child. These activities will benefit their handwriting skills even if they are not using a writing tool.

Hand Strengthening Fun

Children who have weak hands may struggle with activities such as using scissors, grasping a writing utensil, zipping zippers, and maneuvering clothes fasteners. If there is a time your child does not want to write, why not use this as an opportunity to do fun hand strengthening exercises?

Crawling

Crawling is a great way to strengthen hands. It develops fine motor skills and the hand-eye coordination needed for writing. Additionally, it encourages children to use their eyes to track objects, which is needed for children to control what they are drawing or writing. It can sometimes be difficult to get a kid who can walk and run to crawl. Even though crawling is harder for me as an adult than my son, I get on the floor and do it with him. This usually occurs during pretend play or when we role play a story.

As you know, Cory loves the cartoon *Paw Patrol*, and his two favorite dog characters are Chase and Marshall. I will either play Ryder, who assigns the pups tasks to solve problems, or one of the other pups, Rocky. When I play Rocky, we are usually crawling around the house pretending to save cats from trees or cleaning oil off of whales.

Another way I get my son to crawl is when we role play animals. We will play animal exercise videos on YouTube and pretend we are bears, tigers, snakes, crabs, etc. These are great animals to mimic when trying to strengthen the hands. Additionally, one of my son's favorite alphabet books is *Animalphabet* by Julia Donaldson. When we read this book, we act out all the animal characters that represent each letter. This book definitely gives your hands a great workout.

Last, if you have multiple children or a class, doing crawl races is a fun physical activity.

Yoga/Stretching

Yoga is a great exercise to stretch and strengthen hands. Poses like the cobra, salutation seal, and downward-facing dog are fun to do with kids. Yoga also helps to relax them before naps or bedtime. We sometimes do yoga with child exercise groups on YouTube. You can also find recreational centers or yoga studios that offer classes for children.

Rubber Bands

Cory has been fascinated with rubber bands since the first time he saw one. The fact that it stretches and comes in various colors is what drew him in. We also use them for a lot of science experiments we do around the house. If you have young children using rubber bands, please watch them closely. Rubber bands can pop children's skin, and that can be painful.

Rubber bands can be used to create art on geoboards and to learn about math. Geoboards are mathematical manipulatives that help children explore geometric concepts such as area, perimeter, and polygons. It is a board that contains pegs, and kids can stretch rubber bands around them to form line segments and geometric shapes. They also help kids make discoveries about fractions and congruence.

Another fun activity is to get rectangular blocks and plastic cups and have your child wrap rubber bands around them. They can observe how many times certain size rubber bands will fit around the blocks or cups.

Shaping

Shaping is a technique many counselors use to teach kids new behaviors or skills. It allows you to build a desired behavior in children using small steps. Once the child has mastered a step, then you move to the next one.

This technique also requires the adult to provide a reward as the child completes each step to encourage them to go to the next task. An example of a reward could be a praise-specific statement such as, "Good job at putting all your stuffed animals in the toy box." Another example of a reward is telling a child they can play outside once a step is complete.

Shaping provides a great way to set goals as you and your child move along. Also, it requires you to adjust if you see that a child is stuck at one step. Adjusting means you may have to take a break or divide the steps into smaller increments.

Incorporate this strategy to get your children to write for longer periods of time. To do so, you will start by having the child write one letter, word, or sentence. You may also use time; for example, having the child write for one minute. Once they can sit for one minute and write, then next time have them write for one minute and thirty seconds. Keep adding on letters, words, sentences, or time until you have reached a goal with which you are satisfied. After they have accomplished one goal, provide a praise statement or allow them to do their favorite activity.

Another important point is to be patient. Some children learn new behaviors and skills quickly, while others move a little slower.

Below Are More Tips

If your child does not like a certain activity, please adjust. This may look like the following:

- Giving them a break

- Asking them to suggest an activity

- Doing something physical like dancing or going outside to play

- Borrowing an activity from another learning style (discussed in chapter 3)

- Doing an activity that aligns with their interests

Reiterated bonus tip: It is important for your child to see you write. Children pay more attention to what you do than to what you say.

Leading by Example

In our world today, we are constantly using our smartphones and computers to record information. I would type doctor's appointments, grocery lists, and important reminders to myself in the Notes application on my smartphone. Then I noticed Cory watched everything I did. He saw me typing on my phone all the time, so he wanted to do it as well. Whenever he saw the phone, his arms automatically reached out indicating he wanted to use it.

After this realization, I started to write more instead of typing. My grocery lists were written with pen and paper. Outside, I would kneel beside him to draw pictures or write a story, letters, shapes, and numbers. As mentioned before, I wrote during long car trips and doctor's appointments. Sometimes I would randomly pick up his doodle pad and start drawing. Then I noticed as soon as he saw me write, he wanted to do it as well. He started to reach more for crayons and markers instead of my phone.

So let's take on the challenge to physically write more with our children, so they will have more of a desire to do it as well.

Writing that Sparks Your Child's Interest

The great thing about writing is it can be done in various places and on a variety of topics. I try to make writing fun for my son, and something that has helped is to write about topics that interest him. Cory loves to build and race cars, and we often hold competitions around our home. This consists of us racing various cars on the floor. Before we start the race, my son writes a chart with two columns labeled Yellow Car and Blue Car. If the yellow car wins, he will write the word *winner* in its column on the first row. Simultaneously, he will write *loser* in the blue car column in the first row. Another variation is to have the child write the word *fast* for the winning car and *slow* for the losing car. They may repeat these steps after each race.

You can also have a pretend car wash with soapy water in a bin and washcloths. Before washing the cars, help your child create a poster with car wash prices. Your child should write at the top of the poster "Car Wash Prices." Then have them create a chart of the various monetary values. For instance, they may write the following: "Yellow Cars = $2, Blue Cars = $3, and Two Cars = $4." After the sign is complete, use soapy water to wash the cars outside or inside. Get the family involved by having them bring toy cars to get washed. You can take this activity a step further by having the child write receipts after washing each car. Your child can write on the receipt, "Yellow Car = $2, paid in full."

Cory making the car wash prices sign.

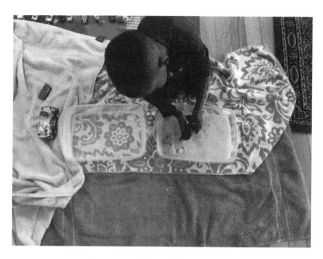

Cory washing his toy cars.

If you have a child that loves to dance, you may have them create a routine and write down the steps. Then have a family member read the dance steps and see if they can do the routine. For the child who loves dolls, you can play Babysitter. Pretend you are going to babysit your child's dolls for five minutes. However, your child must write down what their doll likes to eat and play with. This way you as the babysitter are fully prepared to take on the task.

Be willing to write stories, poems, and raps about anything, such as poop, monsters, unicorns, princesses, your child's favorite cartoon characters, etc. Create a scenario where they are writing but don't realize it because the activity aligns with their interest.

Take a Break

When children want to learn a new concept, they tend to be really focused and in deep concentration. However, when the brain is trying to make connections with a new topic, it needs to go back and forth between focused and diffuse modes. *Diffuse mode* is when your mind is relaxed and not concentrating on anything.[9] Examples of activities that encourage diffuse mode are doodling, taking a walk, looking out the window, daydreaming, or falling asleep.

Have you ever had a problem that you could not figure out how to solve? When you take a break and come back to it, then you can easily solve it. It is because your brain was quietly solving the problem, without you being aware, while in diffuse mode.

Sometimes children get stuck in learning when they don't understand the concept. Other times they get stuck when their brains haven't had the chance to rest. Sometimes they need a break and a chance to get their minds off the problem or situation for a while. This helps to open up their brains to learn. When your child takes a break, ensure it is long enough for them to completely get their minds off the material.

If your child is getting frustrated with writing a letter or number, remember to diffuse and try again at another time. Once they keep

---

[9] Barbara Oakley PhD, Terrane Sejnowski, PhD. "Learning How to Learn: A Guide for Kids and Teens."

going back and forth between focused and diffuse mode, they will eventually be able to write that particular letter or number. Below are more ways to diffuse:

- Playing in or with water
- Playing a sport
- Going for a ride
- Drawing or paint
- Listening to music (without words is best)

Record It

Has your child ever really enjoyed doing something like going to an amusement park or scoring a goal in their soccer game? When a child really has fun doing something, they talk about it repeatedly. It is because they want to hold on to those pleasant memories and feelings. Of course, taking a picture is a wonderful way to remember the fun-filled day. Another way to do this is by writing about it with the Record It activity.

It is better to lead with the Record It activity than wait until the child does not want to write. In other words, make the Record It activity their writing lesson for the day while they are interested. You can print pictures from their favorite events and stick them to a poster or album. Then have your child write captions under the photos. You may also have the child write a short journal they supplement with labeled drawings. Other events they can record are vacations, playdates, eating their favorite food, or some type of accomplishment they are proud of.

Establish a Schedule

Routines and schedules are beneficial to children because they help them understand time management. They also help children feel secure and comfortable because they can predict the next activity and the expectations connected with it. This decreases the frequency of behavior problems.

Choose a time of day when your child is the most alert. It could be in the morning or afternoon when the sun provides natural light. You can also have the child write in the evening as a way to record their favorite times of that particular day. We usually write in the afternoon or evenings when my son has had time during the day to burn energy. Once your child knows it is time to write, most likely their brain will tell their bodies to down settle to focus on writing.

Relax and Be Natural

You don't want to be overbearing when exposing your child to writing. It is best to be natural. This means meeting your child where they are. We know that children naturally like to play and explore, so why not incorporate this into your lessons? Just remember to incorporate natural activities that we mentioned before, like writing your grocery list, notes, daily menu, and important dates or appointments.

Tip: Remember they will eventually learn to write because you are going to use *fun* **in-depth learning to expose your child to writing in many different ways. You may find that you have a child who loves recording their thoughts, activities, and various topics of interests.**

TIP #1

Kids can strengthen their hands by climbing on playground equipment and jungle gyms.

TIP #2

Stirring, kneading, cutting, and scooping are great hand strengthers.

TIP #3

Squeezing bubbles on bubble wrap is fun way to strengthen hands for writing.

CHAPTER 11

What We Do Now

WHAT WE DO NOW

Practice

Although my son knows how to draw shapes and write letters and numbers, we still work at honing his skills. Currently, at the age of four, he enjoys this process because we have found so many ways to make writing fun. He writes on the lined handwriting paper as well as drawing his own straight lines with rulers to create greeting cards. We mix up how and where he writes so the practice of writing does not become boring and monotonous. This is important because he is full of energy and loves to enjoy what he is learning.

In the process of honing his writing skills, he has become creative with where and how he writes. Just this past Sunday, we went to a farm that had various play areas and adventures, such as hay and pony rides, a bamboo maze, goat feeding, and five playgrounds. While waiting for the hayride, he took a stick and started to write in the dirt. I smiled and nodded as he said to me, "You can write anywhere." After the hayride, he picked up a rock to write. He then explained that writing occurs because the rock is separating the dirt to reveal his message. Again, I was glad that he was able to analyze how this works.

Cory making an A on the ground.

The goal should be to try to create a thought in your child's mind that writing can be more than putting pencil to paper. When they think of writing, they should picture painting, sticks, dirt, sand, fingers, shaving cream, sidewalk chalk, cornstarch, etc. All these items have one thing in common: PLAY!

Play

As adults we may go to work every day or stay at home and take care of our kids; however, a child's work is play. Throughout this book, I have given you tons of games/activities and examples of how my son has learned through play. Additionally, playful learning incorporates fun in the day. This why we continue to do it. Let's talk about how my son and I currently participate in playful writing activities.

Automoblox

My son is constantly improving this writing skills by building. As you know, he likes to build letters and numbers with various toys and materials. His favorite activity is building cars and racing them. In my opinion, this has strengthened his hands and given him more control of forming letters and numbers correctly. One toy he likes is *Automoblox* cars, which allow the child to take them apart and change the wheels, rims, tops and front to make a unique style. At first, it was difficult for my son to take the car apart. However, due to practice and the determination to create a car, he is a pro now.

ZOOB Racer

Another toy my son likes is the ZOOB Racer, which contains gears, wheels, and axles that snap, click, and pop together. A child is able to rotate and spin extendable parts to create a design. Just hearing the description of the toy should be an indicator that it is great for the hands and fingers. The ZOOB Racer is for kids six years and older. However, my brother and sister-in-law gave my son this toy when he was three. They love to provide him and me with a challenge. When playing with this toy, I would build most of the car and have him snap a few pieces and read to me how to build it. After playing with this toy more and more, he is able to build an entire car at four years old. Even though this toy was challenging at first, he stuck with it because of his love for cars and racing.

Build-A-Dino

We love science, technology, engineering, art, and math (STEAM) toys because they encourage kids to be hands-on, problem solve, and develop motor skills. All these characteristics can help your child become a great writer. One toy my son plays with is the Build-A-Dino set of three. This toy is for children three and up and includes screwdrivers, nails, and pieces to build the dinosaur. The handling of the screwdriver helps my son with the pincer grasp and hand-eye coordination. The dinosaurs have wheels on the bottom so we can race them after building.

Being Creative

Sometimes I tell Cory to find something to do if I am busy. During these times, I give him the condition of leaving the television off. I purposefully leave safe household materials, such as corks, swim noodles, cotton balls, and toilet paper rolls, at his disposal just to see how he will play with it. One day I saw him build towers of various shapes with the corks. Then he went on to form letters and numbers with them.

After I was done cooking, he asked if I wanted to build with him. I accepted his invitation and then it turned into a race to see who could build a certain shape, letter, or number the fastest. The person who was faster won that particular round. You could incorporate more writing into this activity by helping your child draw a scoreboard to record the winner as you race.

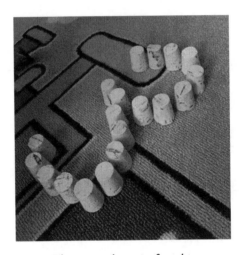

Three made out of corks.

The goal of being creative has decreased my purchase of greeting cards, as I mentioned earlier in the book. Now Cory makes many of the birthday, thank-you, and get-well cards we give people. When Cory is invited to birthday parties, he draws and writes birthday wishes on colorful construction paper. Because he has put time and effort into making the card, he wants to give the birthday girl or boy the card as soon as we arrive to the party. Also, because he is giving these cards to other people, he wants to ensure his letters and numbers are written correctly. He loves to hear feedback from friends, parents, and family members about his cards. This activity is a great motivator to get writing.

Science Experiments

We continue to do science experiments because they are hands-on, improve reading skills, can be messy, and most of all, are fun! Writing is involved when we keep a journal of what happened during the experiments. Your child can draw what happened and then add captions under their pictures. Take the activity a step further by predicting or creating a hypothesis of what you think may happen before doing the experiment. Two recent scientific writing activities that were fun are called Secret Messages and Invisible Ink with Lemon Juice. Instructions for both projects are in the "Activities" section.

Writing Stories

Creating stories is a great motivator for my son to write. However, the stories have to be appealing and entertaining. We usually write about things that interest him, such as cars, playing with friends, skunks, going on adventures, monsters, etc. In order to make the process interactive, we will build the plot together by taking turns writing the next sentence of the story. This is fun because we can play off of each other's creativity. Sometimes I will put a silly sentence in the story just to witness my son's written response. For example, here is a story we wrote in the past.

> *Once there was an elephant named, Ian, who was purple. He wanted to be gray like the other elephants. Ian went to the elephant maker and asked to be gray. The elephant maker made him gray. One day a red lion started running after the elephant family because he was hungry. Ian splashed water on himself to make himself purple again. Ian scared the lion because he was purple. The lion ran away and Ian became the superhero.*

I wrote the sentences about the elephant being purple and the red lion. Cory thought this was funny and was able to keep the plot going.

Our stories are written and created in various places. Our favorite place to write a story is outside with sidewalk chalk. We also have painted stories on big sheets of craft paper and hung them up on the wall. Other ideas are to act out a story and have the other person write what they think your gestures and motions mean. Sometimes we will write about something we have read in the past but change the ending or beginning for a good laugh.

Worksheets

I am not a big proponent of worksheets for young kids; however, we have currently started to use them. My mom and brother gave Cory a workbook because they saw how fast he was progressing with reading, writing, and math. They wanted to ensure that his brain was being stimulated. Even though they are not my favorite, I must admit they provide a guide to what he can learn next. He also likes to do them because the books we use, such as School Zone and Brain Quest books, are colorful and appealing to him. I know it is going well when he requests to do them.

The images on the worksheets are important because a child's brain thinks in colors and pictures. When you ask a child to recall something like their favorite shirt, an image and colors of their shirt pops in their head. The pictures on the worksheet stimulate the child's brain and provide motivation to complete the worksheet. Some schools and parents like to save money by copying the worksheets in black and white. Believe me, I am *not* opposed to saving money. However, if you can, present your child with worksheets with color and pictures. Another idea is to add color to worksheets by coloring the black-and-white pictures or drawing on them.

We usually do two worksheets at a time together. Sometimes, I will create a scenario where we are doing the worksheets together and I don't understand how to do one of the problems. In this instance, Cory will help me with the problem, which gives him confidence. We also figure out how to do the worksheet together. The worksheets give him purpose, in which he is using his writing skills to solve a problem or complete a puzzle. For example, one of the worksheets may ask Cory to help a child name the objects in the picture. Cory may write, "I see a deer. I see a snake." Then I may write a sentence as well just to be involved in the process. This is my approach because my son is still young and I want to make it interactive for him.

How You Can Use This Information

In this book, I have given you a lot of information on how learning to write can be a versatile, interactive, hands-on, and fun experience for your child. I ask that you try these activities with your child little by little and then concentrate on the ones that are appealing to them. Also, don't be afraid to create your own activities! If you bring writing down to their level, learning is inevitable. Thank you for reading!

ACTIVITIES

Challenge to Practice with Fun

- For five days you and your child should think of ways to practice writing in different ways and settings.

- Use the ideas that have been given throughout this book as a starting guide.

I'm Bored

- Allow your child to be bored occasionally.

- Ensure that you have household materials such as paper cups, paper plates, measuring cups, pans, pots, cotton balls.

- Ensure you have writing utensils such as markers, crayons, chalk, paint, etc.

- Let your child be creative.

Secret Message

- Materials needed:
    - Crayons
    - Paper
    - Watercolor paint
    - Water

- ▪ Paintbrushes

- Take a white crayon to write and draw a message on a white piece of paper.

- Have your child take watercolor paint to brush over the paper.

- This will reveal the secret message written by the white crayon.

The mystery message was "I love you."

Mystery Literacy

- ▪ Materials needed:

  - ▪ Lemon

  - ▪ Bowl

  - ▪ Paintbrush or cotton swabs

  - ▪ Paper

  - ▪ An iron

- ▪ Squeeze a lemon into a bowl.

- Use the paintbrush or cotton swab to write a secret message on the paper.

  - Draw quickly to check your work before it dries.

- To reveal the message, the parent should iron the paper with a hot iron until the message is seen.

*Warning: This activity may put brown spots on your iron. In order to clean it, do an Internet search on "how to clean the bottom of an iron."

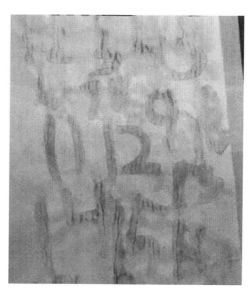

The invisible ink message is numbers 1–16.

After this activity, there were brown spots on my iron. Below is how I cleaned it:

- Materials needed

- Toothpaste

- Baking soda

- Vinegar

- Bowl

- Sponge (with abrasive side)

- Mix toothpaste, baking soda, and vinegar together to make a paste.

- Heat iron to medium.

- Use the abrasive part of the sponge to scrub the bottom of the iron.

  - Make sure not to burn the iron.

- Apply more vinegar if needed.

- Scrub for five minutes.

Writing Stories

- Ask your child to get their favorite object, and then create a story together about it.

- Write two versions of the same story, but make them have different endings.

Colorful Worksheets

- Remember a child's brain thinks in colors and pictures.

- If you are going to use worksheets, ensure they have colorful pictures.

- Add your own color to black-and-white worksheets.

- Be present or do the worksheets with your young child.

- Occasionally pretend you don't understand a problem and have your child explain how to do it.

FAVORITE RESOURCES

Growing Up Reading: Learning to Read through Creative Play by Jill Frankel Hauser

Learning How to Learn by Dr. Barbara Oakley, PhD and Terrence Sejnowski, PhD

The Brave Learner by Julie Bogart

The Three R's by Ruth Beechick

Raising Black Boys by Dr. Jawanza Kunjufu

Mind Maps for Kids by Tony Buzan

Handbook for Raising Black Children: A Comprehensive Guide by Dr. Llaila Afrika

NEXT STEPS

Andrea's Book *Teach Your Toddler to Read Through Play: Over 130 Games/Activities, Tips, and Resources* is available on Amazon

Check out our courses, books, and weekly blog posts.

We have more courses and books coming in the future!

Go to our website, SimplyOutrageousYouth.org and sign into our SOY Resource Library for accelerated fun learning tips for kids!

THANK YOU!

Thank you so much for investing in this book. For more information or further questions, please contact us at SimplyOutrageousYouth.org.